# The Creation
# of Israel

## Titles in the World History Series

The Age of Augustus
The Age of Feudalism
The Age of Pericles
The Alamo
America in the 1960s
The American Frontier
The American Revolution
Ancient Greece
The Ancient Near East
Architecture
The Assyrian Empire
Aztec Civilization
The Battle of the
    Little Bighorn
The Black Death
The Byzantine Empire
Caesar's Conquest of Gaul
The California Gold Rush
The Chinese Cultural
    Revolution
The Civil Rights Movement
The Collapse of the
    Roman Republic
The Conquest of Mexico
The Creation of Israel
The Crimean War
The Crusades
The Cuban Missile Crisis
The Cuban Revolution
The Decline and Fall of the
    Roman Empire
The Early Middle Ages
Egypt of the Pharaohs
Elizabethan England
The End of the Cold War
The French and Indian War
The French Revolution
The Glorious Revolution
The Great Depression
Greek and Roman
    Mythology

Greek and Roman Science
Greek and Roman Theater
The History of Slavery
Hitler's Reich
The Hundred Years' War
The Industrial Revolution
The Inquisition
The Italian Renaissance
The Late Middle Ages
The Lewis and Clark
    Expedition
The Mexican Revolution
The Mexican War of
    Independence
Modern Japan
The Mongol Empire
The Persian Empire
The Punic Wars
The Reformation
The Relocation of the
    North American Indian
The Renaissance
The Roaring Twenties
The Roman Empire
The Roman Republic
Roosevelt and the New Deal
The Russian Revolution
Russia of the Tsars
The Scientific Revolution
The Spread of Islam
The Stone Age
Traditional Africa
Traditional Japan
The Travels of Marco Polo
Twentieth Century Science
The Wars of the Roses
The Watts Riot
Women's Suffrage

**WORLD**
**HISTORY SERIES** ■ ■ ■

# The Creation of Israel

by
Linda Jacobs Altman

Lucent Books, P.O. Box 289011, San Diego, CA 92198-9011

Library of Congress Cataloging-in-Publication Data

Altman, Linda Jacobs, 1943–
    The creation of Israel / by Linda Jacobs Altman.
        p.  cm.—(World history series)
    Includes bibliographical references (p.  ).
Summary: Provides a historical overview of the treatment of
Jews and discusses the role of various individuals and specific
events in leading to the creation of the state of Israel in 1948.
    ISBN 1-56006-288-6 (alk. paper)
    1. Jews—Palestine—History—20th century—Juvenile litera-
ture. 2. Zionism—History—Juvenile literature. 3. Israel—His-
tory—1948–1967—Juvenile literature. [1. Jews—History. 2.
Zionism—History. 3. Israel—History—1948–1967.]
I. Title. II. Series.
DS126.A569      1998
956.94—dc21                                                97-46033
                                                                CIP
                                                                 AC

Copyright 1998 by Lucent Books, Inc., P.O. Box 289011,
San Diego, California 92198-9011

Printed in the U.S.A.

# Contents

| | |
|---|---|
| Foreword | 6 |
| Important Dates in the History of the Creation of Israel | 8 |

**INTRODUCTION**
*Revival in an Ancient Land* — 10

**CHAPTER 1**
*A People Dispossessed* — 13

**CHAPTER 2**
*Theodore Herzl and the Zionist Ideal* — 23

**CHAPTER 3**
*Founders and Pioneers* — 33

**CHAPTER 4**
*Between Two Wars* — 42

**CHAPTER 5**
*No Man's Land* — 53

**CHAPTER 6**
*Fighting for the Dream* — 63

**CHAPTER 7**
*Building a Nation* — 74

**CHAPTER 8**
*Becoming Israeli* — 85

**EPILOGUE**
*The Ongoing Challenge* — 96

| | |
|---|---|
| Notes | 101 |
| For Further Reading | 104 |
| Works Consulted | 105 |
| Index | 107 |
| Picture Credits | 111 |
| About the Author | 112 |

# Foreword

Each year on the first day of school, nearly every history teacher faces the task of explaining why his or her students should study history. One logical answer to this question is that exploring what happened in our past explains how the things we often take for granted—our customs, ideas, and institutions—came to be. As statesman and historian Winston Churchill put it, "Every nation or group of nations has its own tale to tell. Knowledge of the trials and struggles is necessary to all who would comprehend the problems, perils, challenges, and opportunities which confront us today." Thus, a study of history puts modern ideas and institutions in perspective. For example, though the founders of the United States were talented and creative thinkers, they clearly did not invent the concept of democracy. Instead, they adapted some democratic ideas that had originated in ancient Greece and with which the Romans, the British, and others had experimented. An exploration of these cultures, then, reveals their very real connection to us through institutions that continue to shape our daily lives.

Another reason often given for studying history is the idea that lessons exist in the past from which contemporary societies can benefit and learn. This idea, although controversial, has always been an intriguing one for historians. Those who agree that society can benefit from the past often quote philosopher George Santayana's famous statement, "Those who cannot remember the past are condemned to repeat it." Historians who ascribe to Santayana's philosophy believe that, for example, studying the events that led up to the major world wars or other significant historical events would allow society to chart a different and more favorable course in the future.

Just as difficult as convincing students to realize the importance of studying history is the search for useful and interesting supplementary materials that present historical events in a context that can be easily understood. The volumes in Lucent Books' World History Series attempt to present a broad, balanced, and penetrating view of the march of history. Ancient Egypt's important wars and rulers, for example, are presented against the rich and colorful backdrop of Egyptian religious, social, and cultural developments. The series engages the reader by enhancing historical events with these cultural contexts. For example, in *Ancient Greece*, the text covers the role of women in that society. Slavery is discussed in *The Roman Empire*, as well as how slaves earned their freedom. The numerous and varied aspects of everyday life in these and other societies are explored in each volume of the series. Additionally, the series covers the major political, cultural, and philosophical ideas as the torch of civilization is passed from ancient Mesopotamia and Egypt, through Greece, Rome, Medieval Europe, and other world cultures, to the modern day.

The material in the series is formatted in a thorough, precise, and organized manner. Each volume offers the reader a comprehensive and clearly written overview of an important historical event or period. The topic under discussion is placed in a broad historical context. For example, *The Italian Renaissance* begins with a discussion of the High Middle Ages and the loss of central control that allowed certain Italian cities to develop artistically. The book ends by looking forward to the Reformation and interpreting the societal changes that grew out of the Renaissance. Thus, students are not only involved in an historical era, but also enveloped by the events leading up to that era and the events following it.

One important and unique feature in the World History Series is the primary and secondary source quotations that richly supplement each volume. These quotes are useful in a number of ways. First, they allow students access to sources they would not normally be exposed to because of the difficulty and obscurity of the original source. The quotations range from interesting anecdotes to farsighted cultural perspectives and are drawn from historical witnesses both past and present. Second, the quotes demonstrate how and where historians themselves derive their information on the past as they strive to reach a consensus on historical events. Lastly, all of the quotes are footnoted, familiarizing students with the citation process and allowing them to verify quotes and/or look up the original source if the quote piques their interest.

Finally, the books in the World History Series provide a detailed launching point for further research. Each book contains a bibliography specifically geared toward student research. A second, annotated bibliography introduces students to all the sources the author consulted when compiling the book. A chronology of important dates gives students an overview, at a glance, of the topic covered. Where applicable, a glossary of terms is included.

In short, the series is designed not only to acquaint readers with the basics of history, but also to make them aware that their lives are a part of an ongoing human saga. Perhaps they will then come to the same realization as famed historian Arnold Toynbee. In his monumental work, *A Study of History*, he wrote about becoming aware of history flowing through him in a mighty current, and of his own life "welling like a wave in the flow of this vast tide."

# Important Dates in the History of the Creation of Israel

| A.D. | 70 | 1144 | 1648 | 1827 | 1871 | 1884 | 1895 | 1897 | 1903 | 1914 |
|------|----|------|------|------|------|------|------|------|------|------|

**A.D.**

**70**
Imperial Rome puts down Jewish revolt.

**1096**
First Crusade; crusaders attack Jews.

**1144**
First recorded "blood libel" in Norwich, England.

**1264**
Statute of Kalisz protects Polish Jews.

**1648**
Cossacks under Bogdan Chmielnicki slaughter Jews during a revolt against the Polish nobility.

**1804**
Czar Alexander I creates Pale of Settlement.

**1827**
Military conscription of Jews in Russia.

**1860**
Theodore Herzl born May 2 in Budapest, Hungary.

**1871**
Pogrom in Odessa, Russia.

**1882**
Beginning of First Aliyah; Leo Pinsker publishes *Auto-Emancipation*.

**1884**
Pinsker becomes president of Hovevei Zion.

**1894**
Trial of Albert Dreyfus begins December 19.

**1895**
Public degradation of Dreyfus on January 5.

**1896**
Herzl publishes *Der Judenstaat* February 14.

**1897**
First Zionist Congress begins August 29.

**1901**
Jewish National Fund founded.

**1903**
British offer Herzl territory in Uganda.

**1904**
Beginning of Second Aliyah; Herzl dies July 3.

**1914**
World War I begins July 28.

**1917**
Britain issues Balfour Declaration November 2.

**1918   1920   1925   1935   1939   1941   1945   1948   1956   1973**

**1918**
Armistice ends World War I on November 11.

**1919**
Beginning of Third Aliyah.

**1920**
British receive mandate to rule Palestine.

**1924**
Beginning of Fourth Aliyah.

**1925**
World Union of Zionist Revisionists founded.

**1933**
Beginning of Fifth Aliyah.

**1935**
David Ben-Gurion becomes chairman of Jewish Agency.

**1937**
Formation of Irgun paramilitary group.

**1939**
British White Paper of May 17 calls for a combined Jewish-Arab state in Palestine; Germany invades Poland September 1; World War II begins.

**1940**
Founding of Lehi (the Stern Gang).

**1941**
Founding of Palmach strike force.

**1944**
Lehi extremists assassinate Lord Moyne in November.

**1945**
German forces surrender to Allies May 7.

**1946**
Bombing of King David Hotel on July 22.

**1947**
United Nations votes to partition Palestine November 29.

**1948**
Israel declares its independence May 14; War of Independence begins one day later.

**1949**
Israel's first election January 25; Ben-Gurion becomes prime minister.

**1956**
Suez-Sinai War begins October 29.

**1967**
Six-Day War begins June 5.

**1973**
Yom Kippur War begins October 6.

# Revival in an Ancient Land

On November 29, 1947, crowds gathered in the streets of Jerusalem, waiting for an announcement that would change their lives. In New York and Moscow, Paris and London and Rome, people huddled beside their radios, eager to hear what would happen on this historic day. The United Nations was preparing to vote on a plan to divide the ancient land of Palestine into two independent states: one Arab, the other Jewish.

The voting began at 5:00 P.M. It ended with thirty-three nations in favor of partition, thirteen opposed, and ten abstaining. The news rang out over radio stations and public address systems: the Jews once more had a homeland in Eretz Israel (the land of Israel).

*The U.N. conference on November 29, 1947, divided Palestine into separate Jewish and Arab states. The city of Jerusalem became an international zone under U.N. jurisdiction.*

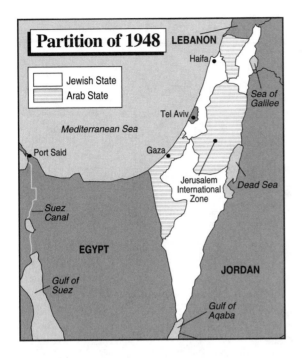

**Partition of 1948**

LEBANON

Jewish State
Arab State

Haifa
Sea of Galilee
Tel Aviv
Mediterranean Sea
Gaza
Port Said
Jerusalem International Zone
Dead Sea
Suez Canal
EGYPT
JORDAN
Gulf of Suez
Gulf of Aqaba

"This is the day that the Lord hath made!" shouted a rabbi in the U.N. delegates' lounge. "Let us be glad and rejoice therein!"[1] In Jerusalem and Tel Aviv, Jewish people cheered and danced and hugged one another in the streets. The religious among them believed that God had given this land to their ancestors nearly five thousand years ago. Now the United Nations was giving it back. For those who celebrated this night, partition came as the fulfillment of a long dream. For 6 million Jewish victims of the Holocaust, it came too late.

Under the dictatorship of Adolf Hitler, a vicious anti-Semite, a vast and efficient Nazi organization exterminated two-thirds of European Jews during World War II (1939–1945). This mass murder became known as the Holocaust. The survivors were left with shattered lives and nightmarish memories. Most of them had no place to go; their homes were gone, their families dead, their futures unthinkably bleak.

The plight of these people nagged at the conscience of the world. For more than fifty years, Zionists (advocates of a Jewish homeland in Palestine) had been trying to establish a Jewish state; it was a matter of survival, they claimed, and the horrors of the Holocaust lent weight to their arguments. The United Nations responded with Resolution 181, establishing partition.

## Arab-Israeli Conflict

Many Zionists were not satisfied with the designated borders nor with the fact that Jerusalem would not be part of the Jewish state. Jerusalem would become an "international city" under U.N. jurisdiction to protect the holy sites of three major religions: Judaism, Christianity, and Islam.

Despite this less-than-perfect arrangement, the Jews accepted the terms of the U.N. resolution. The Arabs did not. How could an international tribunal give away territory it did not own? Palestine was as much an Arabic homeland as a Jewish one, they said, refusing to recognize Israel's right to exist as a nation. Thousands of Arabs lived in the territory that had been handed over to the Jews. What would happen to them?

"I am certain," said Chaim Weizmann, the Zionist statesman who would become Israel's first president, "that the world will judge the Jewish state by what it will do with the Arabs." When discussing future treatment of the Arabs, Weizmann did not mince words:

There must not be one law for the Jews and another for the Arabs. We

*The creation of Israel was met with elation by Jews everywhere. The joy of a new homeland, however, was quickly dampened by strife with neighboring Arabs.*

must stand firm by the ancient principle enunciated in our Torah [the Jewish scriptures]: "One law and one manner shall be for you and for the stranger that sojourneth with you." In saying this, I do not assume that there are tendencies toward inequality or discrimination. It is merely a timely warning which is particularly necessary because we shall have a very large Arab minority.[2]

Statements such as this did not convince the Arabs that they would be secure in a Jewish state. On May 14, 1948, ceremonies in Tel Aviv created a nation and established its first provisional government. The next day, that new nation was at war with its Arab neighbors.

That war ended with a truce, leaving Israel the victor. But the Arab-Israeli conflict did not. It continues to define the social, political, and economic realities of modern Israel and the entire Middle East. The story of that conflict, and of Israel's struggle for national identity, emerges as a compelling sequence of events in twentieth-century history.

# 1 A People Dispossessed

The Jews are an ancient people, tracing their origins back some four thousand years. Their bond to Palestine is rooted deep in their national character and their history. According to Jewish scripture, God promised the land that was then called Canaan to the descendants of Abraham, who were known as "Hebrews" or "Israelites," and later as "Jews."

Every religion has its holy sites; every people, its ancestral homeland. These special places are honored, even revered, but people do not necessarily want to live there. What is different about Israel and the Jews?

Part of the answer to that question lies in the history of the Jewish diaspora (Jewish communities outside of Israel). In 70 A.D., the forces of imperial Rome put down a Jewish rebellion, conquered Jerusalem, and burned its sacred temple. Surviving Jews were driven out of the city and eventually out of the land. They wandered among the nations of the world, settling wherever they were tolerated by the native population.

Some Jews gained acceptance in their host nations, but most kept to themselves, practicing their ancient traditions. They were separate, considered strange—and therefore often regarded as potentially dangerous.

## A Marginal People

In medieval Europe, Jews were marginalized in a number of ways. They were often forbidden to own land, forced to live in certain neighborhoods, restricted to certain occupations. They were reviled as "Christ killers" and given the choice between death or conversion to Christianity.

Some converted, either willingly or merely to save themselves and their families. Most did not. Even in the face of death, they remained staunchly Jewish. Their stubborn refusal to convert threatened many European Christians who needed to believe that theirs was the one true faith.

In the name of that faith, Christian leaders launched the Crusades in 1096. A vast company of noblemen, fortune seekers, adventurers, and common folk set out for Palestine to seize the Christian Holy Land from Muslim rule. Along the way, they frequently murdered unconverted Jews.

Sometimes they enlisted the cooperation of local townsfolk, either directly or by some trick to whip public opinion into a frenzy. In the German city of Worms, enemies of the Jews

took a trampled corpse of theirs, that had been buried thirty days earlier,

## Jews in the First Crusade

*The Jews of the Rhineland were a handy target for Christian crusaders on their way to "liberate" the Holy Land from Muslim control. This sixteenth-century history, quoted in Robert Chazan's* In the Year 1096 . . . the First Crusade and the Jews, *explains how the Jews became victims of overzealous Christians.*

"In the year 1096, Christians gathered from Germany, Italy, France, Spain, and England—more than six hundred thousand warriors—and agreed to ascend to Jerusalem. . . . There befell the Jews in that year . . . decrees and forced conversions in all communities of Germany, France, Spain, England, Italy, Bohemia, and Hungary, decrees the likes of which have never been heard in their harmfulness. Many thousands and ten thousands were slaughtered and killed for the sanctification of the Unique Name [of God]."

*A knight (right) and squire of the First Crusade.*

and carried it through the city, saying: "Behold what the Jews have done to our comrade. They took a gentile [non-Jew] and boiled him in water. They then poured the water into our wells in order to kill us." When the crusaders and burghers [wealthy townsfolk] heard this, they cried out and gathered . . . saying: "Behold the time has come to avenge him who was crucified, whom their ancestors slew. Now let not a remnant or a residue escape; even an infant or a suckling in the cradle."[3]

This incident reflects two myths that were associated with European Jews for years to come: ritual murder and the spread of disease via poisoned water.

When epidemic disease hit an area, frightened people would sometimes imagine that Jews had placed some deadly substance into the wells. Rarely did anyone notice that Jews were dying as readily as Christians.

The first recorded ritual murder charge occurred in 1144 in Norwich, England. When a Christian boy named William disappeared, the townsfolk spread a terrible story about his fate. The Jews had killed him, they said; "everybody knew" that Jews used the blood of Christian children in their rites.

"Blood libel," as it was called, was frequently discussed by Christians around the Jewish holiday of Passover. Christians thought that Jews needed fresh blood as an ingredient in matzo, the flat, unleavened bread used during that holiday. Because Jews were considered so dangerous, making them easily recognizable became a matter of Christian self-defense.

## Marking the Jews

In 1215, Pope Innocent III decreed that all Jews should wear a "yellow badge of shame"[4] on their breasts, to identify themselves as Jews. "Moreover, they shall not walk out in public on the Days of Lamentation [grief] or the Sunday of Easter; for as we have heard, certain ones among them do not blush to go out on such days more than usually ornamented."[5]

In 1248, Louis IX of France ordered Jews to wear a second badge on the back of their outer garments "so that those who were thus marked might be recognized on every side."[6] In many places, both men and women were required to wear a "Jew's hat" along with the badge. The hat was often pointed like a traditional dunce cap, designed to make the wearer look ridiculous as well as to identify him or her as a Jew.

Jews had to defer to Christian people, Christian places, and Christian observances. They could not speak of their religion, but Christians could pressure them to convert and to be baptized. This pressure could take many forms, ranging from humane and respectful attempts at persua-sion to the brutal convert-or-die methods of the crusaders.

In 1269, a converted Jew who had taken the name "Paul Christian" convinced Louis IX of France that the way to convert Jews was to win them to the faith by persuasive preaching. As Jews would not voluntarily listen to Christian sermons, the king issued a proclamation requiring them to attend conversionary sermons. Like other such efforts, this one was a general failure. Jews attended, listened politely, and went their way—unconverted and unmoved.

One result of discriminatory measures against Jews was to transform their neighborhoods into pockets of poverty. To be a Jew in medieval Europe was to struggle endlessly. A bright young Jew could not aspire

*King Louis IX, shown here kneeling before the cross while angels look on, ordered Jews in his realm to wear identifying badges and attend Christian sermons.*

to a good education and a well-paying professional career. An elderly Jew could claim no financial security in his last years.

Jews had to survive in jobs that Christians did not want; by and large, this meant monetary occupations. The medieval church would not allow Christians to lend money at interest. To do so was called *usury,* and it was a mortal sin. Jews stepped into the breech, becoming itinerant peddlers, moneylenders, pawnbrokers, even international financiers. For this, they were scorned as money grubbers by the Christian world.

Since Jews were considered dishonest schemers, cheating a Jew or reneging on (ignoring) a debt was both acceptable and frequently encouraged. Jewish historian Nathan Ausubel wrote:

Quite frequently, the contract between a Jewish moneylender and an individ-

## Jews and the Black Death

*When the plague hit Europe in 1348, so many terrified people blamed the Jews that Pope Clement VI issued a statement on September 26, 1348. Clement's statement is quoted in Alexis P. Rubin's* Scattered Among the Nations.

"Lately there has come to Our hearing the fame, or more precisely the infamy, that certain Christians, seduced by that liar the devil, are imputing to poisonings by Jews the pestilence with which God is afflicting the Christian people. For He is outraged by the sins of this people who, acting on their own temerity, and taking no account of age or sex, have impiously annihilated some from among the Jews. . . . Now, if the Jews were guilty, their conscience burdened by a crime so great, We would wish them struck by a penalty of suitable severity—although a sufficient one could hardly be conceived. Still, since this pestilence, all but universal everywhere, by a mysterious judgement of God has afflicted, and does now afflict . . . both Jews and many other nations to whom life in common with Jews is unknown, that the Jews have provided the occasion or the cause for such a crime has no plausibility."

*A medieval illustration of a plague victim.*

ual ruler or a municipality . . . [often] turned out to be merely of one-sided benefit. . . . Common enough . . . was the practice of some ruling princes who, wishing to curry favor with their subjects . . . would declare a general moratorium on all debts to Jewish moneylenders.[7]

Every time the Jews thought they had found a haven, a homeland, the political situation would change and they once more became outcasts. No matter how promising the situation, hatred seemed to lurk beneath the surface, ready to erupt at any time.

## Jews in Medieval Poland

The Jewish presence in eastern Europe started off on the best of terms. In the thirteenth century, when Jews were being expelled from one western European nation after another, King Boleslav of Poland offered them sanctuary.

Medieval Poland had neither developed a reliable currency nor escaped the cumbersome feudal system; a handful of aristocrats ruled the kingdom while the common folk lived in severe poverty. Ongoing warfare with the Tartars had drained the national treasury. Boleslav believed that Jews, with their experience in commerce and finance, could revitalize the economy. To encourage them to immigrate, he set forth the historic Statute of Kalisz in 1264, giving Jews freedom of worship and liberal protection under the law. Seventy years later, King Casimir III

extended the rights, privileges, and protections granted to the Jews by the

*This medieval Jewish man (center) wears the characteristic pointed hat and carries a money pouch. Jews assumed the occupations deemed undesirable by Christians, such as moneylending.*

Statute of Kalisz. Most of those included in his charter of 1334 were of an economic nature. However—and most important of all—he granted to the Jews a greater measure of communal self-rule . . . than they had ever enjoyed before in the Polish lands. This proved most significant for the continuity of Jewish ethnic, religious, and cultural life in Poland.[8]

This happy state of affairs did not last. By the fifteenth century, ritual murder accusations were being made throughout the kingdom. Polish Jews found themselves in mortal danger as superstitious and fearful peasants launched attacks against them:

During Easter Week of 1407, when the religious hysteria awakened by the memories of the Crucifixion became most acute, a mob of looters and cutthroats . . . led by a local priest, roared through the Cracow ghetto, sparing the lives only of those who promptly submitted to baptism. This choice offered the Jew—"Baptism or death"—became the tragic pattern for the centuries which followed.[9]

That pattern was never more deadly than in 1648, when the cossack (peasant-warrior) Bogdan Chmielnicki led a revolt against the Polish nobility. This uprising, like the culture that produced it, divided people into two categories: the peasantry and the nobility. Jews found themselves squeezed in the middle. The nobility had no particular loyalty to them. They were outsiders, a people of strange customs and even stranger religious belief.

Chmielnicki and his cossacks hated Jews almost as much as they hated the nobility. They considered Jews to be agents of an oppressive social system: collecting taxes, lending money, and making the feudal economy work. For this role, tens of thousands of Jews were slaughtered by marauding cossacks. According to some estimates, between two hundred thousand and four hundred thousand Jews died in eighteen months of cossack terror.

The survivors of Chmielnicki's attack became even more isolated from the Christian majority. They pulled together tightly in defense against a hatred they could neither understand nor control. That isolated Jewish world of seventeenth-century Poland produced a sect called the *Chasidim* (the pious folk). Theirs was a faith of joy and song, of spiritual dance and ultimate rapture. Their leader, known as the Baal Shem Tov (master of the good name), taught that God was present in every moment, every event of life. It was therefore the duty of the faithful to rejoice in that presence, regardless of outward circumstances.

To well-educated Jews, Chasidim might have seemed simplistic and hopelessly naive, but it comforted the common folk and gave them the strength to survive in a world that hated and feared them. Unfortunately, it also increased both their isolation from the gentile world and their strangeness.

## In Darkest Russia

In the late eighteenth century, Russia conquered most of Poland, Lithuania and Ukraine, acquiring in the process some nine hundred thousand Jewish inhabitants, most of whom lived in impoverished shtetls (Yiddish for "small towns"). Their life was hard and demanding; they always seemed to be just one step ahead of starvation, scratching out their livelihoods as shopkeepers, craftsmen, or traveling peddlers. Neither the Russian nobility nor the Orthodox Christian clergy knew what to do with them.

Catherine the Great dealt with the problem by forbidding Jews to live outside existing Jewish communities. Czar Alexander I formalized this prohibition in 1804, officially creating the Pale of Settlement, an area of twenty-five provinces in western Russia where Jews were allowed to live. Any Jew wishing to travel outside the Pale needed special permission from the government.

When Czar Alexander I (ruled 1801–1825) came to the throne, he established new, liberal policies for the common folk of Russia, including Jews. With a single decree, Alexander placed Jews on par with gentiles; they could own land and farm it, follow any trade, and attend any school they wished. Sadly, the improved conditions did not last for long.

Alexander became fearful that a taste of freedom would only whet people's appetite for more, which could lead to revolution. The realization terrified Alexander, who soon repealed all his reforms.

When Nicholas I assumed the throne in 1823, he heaped additional hardships upon the Jews. He cast them out of the Grodno and Kiev Districts, and from all settlements on the Black and Baltic Seas. Thousands of desperately poor Jews crowded into what remained of the Pale. Many of these refugees became *luftmenschen* (men of air), people with no steady work, no assets, and no realistic chance of bettering their lot.

In 1827, Nicholas instituted compulsory military service for Jewish males between the ages of twelve and eighteen. These boys could be kept in the army for twenty-five years, essentially a lifetime. Most who were taken never saw their families again. Jewish parents hid their sons, disguised them as

*Czar Alexander I granted rights to Jews equal to those of the Christian common folk of Russia. Fearing revolution, though, he quickly repealed the new policies.*

girls, even lamed them in the hope that they would be rejected by the military.

According to historian Nathan Ausubel, there was a plan behind this policy, and it had as much to do with turning Jewish boys into Christians as turning them into soldiers:

> By tearing [boys] away . . . from their families and their Jewish religious environment . . . they would become weaned from their identity . . . [and] so Russified that they would be more amenable to efforts to convert them to the Russian Orthodox faith.[10]

Military conscription was only the beginning of anti-Jewish policies so harsh that the phrase "in darkest Russia" became a common figure of speech in several languages. Fanatical Russian nationalists known as the Black Hundreds exalted the name and fame of "Holy Mother Russia" by trying to liquidate the Jews.

The first *pogrom* (organized massacre) occurred in 1871 in the city of Odessa. After that, the horror became almost routine: mounted troops would swoop down on a Jewish neighborhood, putting shops and homes to the torch; men, women, and children to the sword.

A decade later, Alexander III followed his coronation with a massive pogrom in the town of Elizavetgrad, then with a rash of actions in every part of the Pale. This terrorism led to the May Laws of 1882, named for the month they went into force.

The May Laws destroyed the Jews economically, placing them under so many restrictions that simply earning a living became nearly impossible. Jews who could scrape together enough money for passage fled Russia in a mass migration that historian Nathan Ausubel compared to the great biblical exodus from Egypt. Between 1880 and 1914, about 2.6 million Russian and eastern European Jews sought a better life in western Europe and the United States.

*This engraving captures the terror and chaos as Jews are violently driven from their homes in nineteenth-century Russia.*

## Liberty! Equality! Fraternity!

In the West, human rights had moved to the forefront of political life. The American and French revolutions had spread the ideas of liberty, equality, and fraternity to people of all social classes and religious persuasions. Absolute monarchies crumbled, or were transformed into more democratic constitutional monarchies.

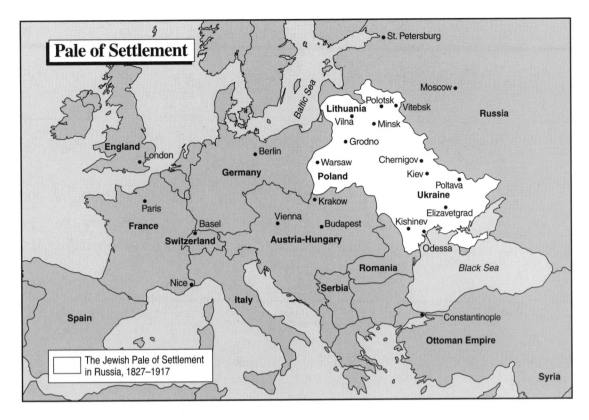

**Pale of Settlement**

St. Petersburg

Moscow

Polotsk · · Vitebsk
**Lithuania**
Vilna · · Minsk
**Russia**

· Grodno

· Warsaw   Chernigov ·
**Poland**   Kiev ·
· Poltava
**Ukraine**
· Krakow   Elizavetgrad ·
Vienna   Kishinev ·
· Budapest
Odessa ·

Baltic Sea

**England**
London ·

· Berlin
**Germany**

**France**
Paris ·
Basel ·
**Switzerland**

Nice ·

**Italy**

**Spain**

**Austria-Hungary**

**Romania**   *Black Sea*
**Serbia**

Constantinople ·

**Ottoman Empire**

**Syria**

The Jewish Pale of Settlement
in Russia, 1827–1917

Jews were included in this great human rights upheaval. One nation after another emancipated its Jewish population: France in 1791, Prussia (later part of Germany) in 1812, England in 1860, Italy in 1870. After generations of living as strangers, Jews seemed to be on the brink of belonging. Many stood ready to take their places as full partners in society. Others were not so sure. Watch out, they warned; take it slow. Remember the lessons of history.

Unfortunately, these naysayers were right. Emancipation provoked a serious backlash, a new excuse for hating Jews. In 1879, German journalist Wilhelm Marr coined the term *anti-Semitism* to describe this hatred, which was based on false ideas of race. In particular, he drew on the work of Arthur de Gobineau, whose "Essay on

the Inequality of the Human Races" explained why some races were supposedly inferior to others. He called the Semites (Jews) a debased "mongrel race" and extolled the so-called Aryans as the superrace that created Western civilization. Actually, both "Aryan" and "Semitic" originally described language groupings; they had nothing to do with race.

Nevertheless, Wilhelm Marr picked up these terms and made them his own, claiming that the Germanic or Nordic peoples were direct descendants of the Aryans. They were therefore superior to all other peoples, especially the Jews. Marr founded the League of Anti-Semitism as a forum for his ideas.

In advancing his racial theories, Marr faced one strange problem: these so-called

*A page from a German children's book published in 1936 compares the physical traits of a German (left) and a Jew. Anti-Semites believed that Germanic people were racially superior to Jewish people.*

inferior Jews were making the most of their emancipation. Historian Alexis P. Rubin made these observations:

> By the 1870s, Germany's Jews, although a small minority of the country's population, were well represented in banking, journalism, law, and medicine. They were professors and school teachers, artists, musicians, actors, novelists. Talented, liberal, innovative, quite a few became very successful. Many Germans, especially from the lower middle class, deeply resented what they believed . . . was the "Judification" of their country. These people accepted the new racial theories which said Jews were inferior. Yet somehow Jews had risen to the pinnacles of success in German art, science, and business. How could this be so? The anti-Semites had a ready answer: Jews, by blood, were conspiratorial, grasping, greedy, and their ultimate aim was world domina-

tion. Against such a foe even the Aryan master race faced defeat.[11]

To imperial Rome the Jews had been a political and military problem. To the medieval church, they were "Christ killers" and unbelievers. Their very existence challenged the notion that Christianity was the one true faith for all of humankind. Jews who clung to their ancestral faith could expect trouble; those who converted could generally expect full acceptance from the Christian community.

The new racial definition of Jewishness triggered a new hatred. Racist anti-Semitism placed Jewishness "in the blood." Neither Christian baptism nor German patriotism could transform a Jew into anything but a Jew. This racist vision would one day enable Nazi Germany to plot the total destruction of European Jews. It would also make the creation of a sovereign (independent, self-governing) Jewish state into a matter of survival.

# Chapter

# 2 Theodore Herzl and the Zionist Ideal

Zionism began as a response to the dangerous undercurrent of racism that tainted Jewish emancipation in Europe. Since their final dispersion in 70 A.D., Jews had dreamed of returning to their homeland. For the most part, it was just that: a dream. Each spring at Passover, Jews celebrated their ancestors' freedom from slavery in Egypt. They would tell the ancient story at the Seder (ritual meal) and comfort one another with the vow "next year in Jerusalem."

Hundreds of "next years" passed, and still Jews celebrated Passover in the lands of the diaspora and longed for Eretz Israel (the land of Israel). In the nineteenth century that spiritual longing became a political goal, and Jews began looking toward Palestine as the country of their future as well as the homeland of their past.

## The Birth of an Idea

Early Zionism was more intellectual theory than practical plan. In western Europe,

## The Pale of Settlement

*Russia dealt with its Jews by isolating them in a specific territory —the Pale of Settlement—where grinding poverty was the norm. Israeli writer Amos Elon described the Pale in his book* The Israelis: Founders and Sons.

"A traveler making his way through European Russia during the last half of the nineteenth century viewed a strangely gray, desperately backward, sorely depressing, monotonous land. . . . The northwestern belt between Warsaw, Minsk, and Vitebsk, which at that time was one of the main population centers of world Jewry, was an immense lowland of forest and marsh with patches of primitive cultivation in between. As it rose almost imperceptibly toward the Urals [mountain range] in the east, it was all flatness and seemingly unlimited space, dull and inert."

one of the earliest theorists was Moses Hess (1812–1875), a socialist who called for a secular (nonreligious) communal society of Jews in Palestine. In his 1862 book *Rome and Jerusalem,* he stated that the Jews "should make every effort to . . . achieve the political restoration of the land of Israel." According to the distinguished Jewish writer Chaim Potok, Hess wanted this future Jewish state

> to be based on land acquired by the entire people; on a legal framework that would enable labor to proceed fruitfully; and on societies of agriculture, trade and industry.[12]

*Rome and Jerusalem* was ahead of its time; the Jewish masses did not know it existed, and the Jewish intelligentsia (intellectuals) did not seem to care. It was a failure in its day, selling just two hundred copies. Hess had no way of knowing that the ideas in this publicly unsuccessful book would one day be given life by the great Zionist organizer Theodore Herzl.

Some years after *Rome and Jerusalem* had quietly appeared on the scene, Peretz Smolenskin (1842–1885), editor of a Hebrew literary magazine in Vienna, published "The Eternal People." In this essay, he joined the call for a new Jewish presence in Palestine. This reborn nation would become a dynamic center for Jewish intellectual values. Free from discriminatory policies and second-class citizenship, Jewish intellectuals and artists could reach their full potential.

Like Moses Hess before him, Smolenskin saw his work largely ignored by western European Jews. Theirs was a polite, increasingly tolerant world; in time they would blend into it completely. Believing this, western Jews were not eager to surrender their hard-won comfort for an uncertain future in Palestine.

## The New Yishuv

For Russian Jews the situation was different. They faced vicious persecution, unrelenting poverty, and a growing desire to escape the nightmare their lives had become. For them, Zionism was not a political question; it was a matter of survival.

Russian Zionism began at the grassroots level. All over the Pale, Jews formed Hovevei Zion (lovers of Zion) groups, and planned to establish pioneering colonies in Palestine. Between 1882 and 1903, a handful of Jewish settlers left Russia to launch the first *aliyah* (the Zionist term for immigration to Palestine).

These pioneers found a land that was not entirely empty of Jews; perhaps five thousand lived there. They had come as spiritual seekers, not as settlers. Some spent their time in study and prayer; some merely waited to die in the land they called holy. These were the people of what came to be called the "old Yishuv" (Jewish community in Palestine). The new Yishuv, represented by the youthful pioneers, had more worldly goals. They wanted to establish Jewish settlements and build Jewish farms.

They soon learned that reaching those goals would not be easy. Under the rule of the Ottoman Empire (present-day Turkey) Palestine had languished. Reviving it would not be a simple task. Political scientist Mark Tessler wrote:

> Life in the new Yishuv was difficult . . . with agricultural communities in particular experiencing serious problems

## Russian Anti-Semitism

*In his book*
Antisemitism: Its
History and Causes,
*Bernard Lazare
described the way in
which czarist Russia
used anti-Semitism to
serve its own ends:*

"What are then the real causes of antisemitism? They are political and religious. . . . The Russian people, laden with misery, crushed under taxes . . . with suffering and humiliation is in an unbearable condition. Generally resigned, they are liable to yield to passions; their uprisings and revolts are formidable; antisemitic riots are the proper thing to divert popular anger, and that is why the government encouraged them and often provoked them."

*Russian police watch as Jews are tormented during a pogrom. The government condoned such violence against Jews as a means of diverting public anger away from the government.*

during the early years of their existence. Most Jewish immigrants were poorly prepared for farming. Nor were they aided by the harsh conditions prevailing where many of their settlements were located. Some for a time lived in caves, and many fell ill, often from malaria.[13]

## Do-It-Yourself Freedom

In the same year those first Hovevei Zion colonists arrived in Palestine, physician Leo Pinsker (1821–1891) published a Zionist pamphlet entitled *Auto-Emancipation.* The underlying reason for anti-Semitism, Pinsker contended, was the peculiar status of Jews among the peoples of the world. Diaspora Jews were not simply members of a minority religious group; they were a nation without a homeland.

Gentiles had separate national and religious identities: being a Christian did not stop a person from also being a German, a Frenchman, or a Russian, for example. In the eyes of many gentiles, Jews could not maintain this dual identity. They were Jews, first, last, and always; living on the fringes of other nations, their loyalties always suspect.

Not until the Jewish people had a politically secured territory would the problem disappear, said Pinsker. His diagnosis of the "Jewish problem" was forceful, but his solution was vague. Saying that the Jews needed a homeland was one thing; explaining how they should go about getting it was quite another.

Even without a political action strategy, *Auto-Emancipation* inspired Jews who longed to escape pogroms, discrimination, and the grinding poverty of the Pale. In 1884, Hovevei Zion groups from all over Russia gathered at a conference. They discussed ways to recruit Jewish settlers for Palestine and to support the settlements that were already there. This piecemeal approach fell short of Dr. Pinsker's nationalistic vision, but he was powerless to change it. Alex Bein, writing in his biography of Theodore Herzl, commented,

> The energies of the [Hovevei Zion] expended themselves in the collection of [small] sums of money for the support of the colonies in Palestine, and these minor labors gradually pushed into the background the great concepts on which the colonization had originally been founded.[14]

Most of the colonies of the first aliyah failed to become self-sustaining. Hundreds of settlers lost heart and returned to Russia. Others left their agricultural colonies to scrape out a living in the cities of Palestine. A few became gentlemen farmers, buying cheap land and hiring laborers to do the work.

Pinsker was not the only member of Hovevei Zion who was unhappy with the colonization efforts. In 1889, an article entitled "This Is Not the Way" appeared in a Hebrew language magazine. This article was the first in a lengthy series of commentaries on the activities of Hovevei Zion, written under the byline Ahad Ha'am, which means "One of the People."

Ahad (real name, Asher Ginzberg) criticized Hovevei Zion for treating Palestine as a haven for downtrodden Jews. The organization should be more than that, he said; it should be a vibrant center for the rebirth of national spirit and Jewish culture. Only in this way could it become the focal point for world Jewry.

In 1890, Ahad Ha'am was elected to the executive committee of Hovevei Zion. According to Alex Bein, Ahad represented the "cultural factor," while Hovevei Zion president, M. L. Lilienblum, dealt with the practical concerns of buying land and building colonies, and Rabbi Samuel Mohilever protected the Jewish religious heritage.

Because these early Zionists lacked clear goals for the new Palestinian colonies, the Zionist movement floundered. Dr. Leo Pinsker died in 1891, a disappointed man who had watched his vision wither from lack of direction. Wrote Alex Bein:

> The great national political idea faded into the background, retaining some of its original force only among the youth, to whom it served as a romantic vision. A few years more and the entire movement seemed doomed to extinction.[15]

At this low point, Hungarian leader Theodore Herzl burst upon the Zionist scene. Tall and handsome, with refined manners and a commanding presence, Herzl had always worn his Jewishness lightly. He believed that assimilation was the answer to Europe's so-called Jewish question. Given time, Jews would blend into the surrounding culture and anti-Semitism would promptly disappear. A military scandal changed his mind.

## Anti-Semitism and the Dreyfus Affair

In December 1894, Herzl became interested in the court martial of a French army officer charged with treason. Captain Alfred Dreyfus was a native-born Frenchman and a Jew, with an exemplary military record. Despite shaky evidence and witnesses who were less than credible, he was convicted of selling military secrets to Germany. Dreyfus was sentenced to life imprisonment on the infamous Devil's Island.

During the trial, Jews were attacked in the streets and insulted in the press. Jewish schoolchildren were taunted by their gentile classmates. On the day Alfred Dreyfus was ceremonially stripped of his rank and paraded in disgrace before his former comrades, an unruly crowd gathered to witness the proceedings. "Death to Dreyfus," some of them shouted, and "death to traitors." Then voice after voice raised a new cry: "death to Jews." Herzl wrote:

*Early Zionist Theodore Herzl initially believed that assimilation of Jews into local cultures would rid society of anti-Semitism.*

The Dreyfus case . . . embodies the desire of the vast majority of the French to condemn a Jew, and to condemn all Jews in this one Jew. Death to the Jews! howled the mob, as the decorations were being ripped from the captain's coat. . . . Where? In France. In republican, modern, civilized France, a hundred years after the Declaration of the Rights of Man. The French people, or at any rate the greater part of the French people, does not want to extend the rights of man to Jews. The edict of the great Revolution has been revoked.[16]

Herzl decided that his dream of full assimilation was just that: a dream. European Jews would never merge into the gentile mainstream. Some might bridge the gulf, but most would find the doors forever barred. This realization became a defining moment for Herzl. He had gone to the trial for a news story but found a life work instead.

Alfred Dreyfus was eventually cleared of the charges against him and freed from prison, but that did not change Herzl's commitment to Jewish nationhood. After Dreyfus's degradation, Herzl returned to Vienna where he made his home. There, he refined his ideas and began the often-discouraging process of trying to gain the support of influential Jews.

The philanthropist and railroad businessman Moritz de Hirsch disliked Herzl's plan to reeducate oppressed Jews to become "strong for war, filled with the joy of work, penetrated by high virtues."[17] That would be a terrible mistake, Hirsch claimed. The problem with Jews was that they aimed too high: "My aim is to discourage this pushfulness among the Jews. They mustn't make such great progress. All the

# The Degradation of Alfred Dreyfus

*On January 5, 1895, the French Army stripped Captain Alfred Dreyfus of his rank. The incident was a turning point for Theodore Herzl, who wrote about the ceremony at which the commanding general of the Paris garrison ripped the rank insignia off Dreyfus's uniform to the roll of military drums. Herzl's description of the event is excerpted from his biography written by Alex Bein.*

"Then began the parade of the condemned before the troops. Dreyfus marched along the sides of the square like a man who knows himself to be innocent. . . . At twenty minutes past nine the parade was over. Dreyfus was then handcuffed and given into the custody of the gendarmes. . . . There was a curious excitement amongst those who had been able to witness the ceremony of the degradation. The strange, firm bearing of the prisoner had made a profound impression on some of them."

*Flanked by soldiers and stripped of his rank, Alfred Dreyfus is marched in front of troops in Paris after being convicted of treason.*

*Alfred Dreyfus's treason case triggered a rash of anti-Semitism in France, prompting Zionists to reassert the need for a Jewish nation.*

hatred of us comes from this."[18] Herzl was stunned by this reaction from a Jew who had become all the things he now criticized. He made no more attempts to convince Hirsch.

## Laying the Foundation of Political Zionism

In the privacy of his study Herzl continued to formulate his plan. The idea of a reborn Jewish nation consumed him, as he wrote in his diary:

> For some time now I have been engaged in a work of indescribable greatness. It has assumed the aspect of some powerful dream. But days and weeks have passed since it has filled me utterly, it has overflown into my unconscious self, it accompanies me wherever I go, it broods above all [ordinary] conversation . . . it disturbs me and intoxicates me. What it will lead to is impossible to surmise as yet. But my experience tells me that it is something marvelous, even as a dream, and that I should write it down—Title: "The Promised Land."[19]

It was about the need for a Jewish state—a homeland that Jews could call their own.

In his ongoing effort to find powerful allies, Herzl organized his thoughts and committed them to paper in an essay entitled, "An Address to the Rothschilds." Like Hirsch, the Rothschilds were Jews who had acquired wealth and power in a gentile world. The Rothschild banking fortune was well known throughout Europe. So was the Rothschild commitment to supporting Jewish causes. Their backing could make the difference between success and failure for a fledgling Jewish state.

As a test Herzl showed the essay to his longtime friend Friedrich Schiff. To his dismay, Schiff called it the "product of an overstrained mind"[20] and suggested that Herzl seek immediate medical treatment. This reaction from a trusted friend all but destroyed Herzl's confidence, if not in the idea, then in his ability to see it through.

Fortunately for the Zionist movement, Herzl drew strength from the power of his vision; he would not rest until he had seen it through. Just when he was most in need of a strong ally, he showed his essay to Max Nordau, a physician and writer eleven years older than Herzl. Nordau, too, had witnessed the degradation of Alfred Dreyfus and understood its anti-Semitic nature. When he read the "Address," his reaction was stronger than Herzl had dared to hope. "If you are mad, we are mad together!" he exclaimed. "Count on me, I am with you!"[21]

Next to come aboard was British-Jewish novelist Israel Zangwill. Herzl and Zangwill met in London in November 1895. The conference was not easy for either man. Herzl spoke German and French, but little English; Zangwill spoke only English. Despite these difficulties, the novelist was impressed with his visitor. He introduced Herzl to a number of influential Jews, including the membership of the Maccabeans, a Jewish businessmen's group. They listened attentively. At last Herzl had found some Jews who would take him seriously.

Successful as it was, the London trip showed Herzl that recruiting allies a few at a time would never produce the great support the project needed. For that, he would have to reach people by the thousands. In 1890s Europe, the only way to do that was to write a book.

## Reaching the People

On February 14, 1896, Herzl's *The Jewish State: An Attempt at a Modern Solution of the Jewish Question* was published in German by M. Breienstein, a Viennese bookseller and publisher. Herzl's vision provoked immediate response from all over Europe, not all of it favorable.

Writer Stefan Zweig was still in high school when *Der Judenstaat* (the German title of Herzl's book) appeared:

> I can still remember the general astonishment and annoyance of the middle class Jewish elements of Vienna. What has happened, they said angrily, to this otherwise intelligent, witty, and cultivated writer? What foolishness is this that he thought up and writes about? Why should we go to Palestine? Our language is German and not Hebrew, and beautiful Austria is our home. . . . Why does he, who speaks as a Jew and who wishes to help Judaism, place arguments in the hands of our worst enemies and attempt to separate us, when every day brings us more closely and intimately into the German world?[22]

The Rothschild reaction was just as negative. After months of trying, Herzl finally had an interview with Baron Edmond de Rothschild in Paris. The Baron scorned the whole idea of Jewish statehood—ridiculous, he called it. Only the poorest,

*Max Nordau, a German physician and author, was a staunch supporter of Theodore Herzl and his vision of a Jewish state.*

*Many Zionists were deeply concerned about preserving Jewish ideals and allowing those ideals to shape a nation. In 1934, when anti-Semitism was on the rise in Germany, Albert Einstein reflected upon the nature of Jewish values in his book* Ideas and Opinions.

"The pursuit of knowledge for its own sake, an almost fanatical love of justice and the desire for personal independence—these are the features of the Jewish tradition which make me thank my lucky stars that I belong to it.

Those who are raging today against the ideals of reason and individual liberty and are trying to establish a spiritless state-slavery by brute force rightly see in us their irreconcilable foes. History has given us a difficult row to hoe; but so long as we remain devoted servants of truth, justice, and liberty, we shall continue not merely to survive as the oldest of living peoples, but by creative work to bring forth fruits which contribute to the ennoblement of the human race, as heretofore."

least educated Jews would leave Europe for an uncertain future in the Middle East. Such people would not be able to support themselves, let alone build a nation. The baron wanted nothing to do with such a farfetched scheme.

Herzl's most enthusiastic support came from eastern Europe and the Pale. In the work of this elegant journalist from Vienna, the members of Hovevei Zion saw a focused program that could give new purpose to their movement. Chaim Weizmann wrote:

> It was an utterance which came like a bolt from the blue. Fundamentally, *The Jewish State* contained not a single new idea for us. . . . Not the ideas, but the personality which stood behind them appealed to us. Here was daring, clarity, and energy. The very fact that the Westerner came to us unencumbered by our own preconceptions had its appeal. We were right in our instinctive appreciation that what had emerged from the *[The Jewish State]* was less a concept than a historic personality.[23]

Such was the force of this "historic personality" that the newborn Zionist movement was ready for its first congress in the late summer of 1897.

# 3 Founders and Pioneers

Building on the interest aroused by his book, Theodore Herzl set to work translating words into actions. On August 29, 1897, he assembled the First Zionist Congress at a concert hall in Basel, Switzerland. More than two hundred delegates attended, along with dozens of newspaper reporters and a number of gentile dignitaries. By the standards of its day, the congress was quite a media event, as well as a planning session for a new political movement.

## The First Zionist Congress

With an unerring sense of public drama, Herzl had insisted that all delegates dress formally in knee-length dress coats and white ties. At one side of the podium hung a white flag with two blue stripes and a blue, six-pointed Star of David.

Three taps of a gavel opened the session. Dr. Carpel Lippe moved to the podium, covered his head, and recited the Hebrew prayer Shehechiyanu: "Blessed are you, Lord our God . . . who has kept us in life, has sustained us, and has permitted us to reach this moment."[24] This is the Jewish prayer of arrival, uttered for significant personal and community events such as religious celebrations, birthdays, or taking

possession of a new home. In Basel, it brought tears to the eyes of many delegates and absolute silence to the hall.

When Herzl stepped to the platform, the delegates jumped to their feet and cheered. It was a grand beginning for the new organization. In the three days of that first congress, the delegates created an organization based on Herzl's guidelines in *Der Judenstaat*. A statement of Zionist objectives, which came to be known as the Basle Program, laid the foundation for the future of the movement. The Zionist Organization would unify Jews from all over the diaspora and act as their legal representative; a separate division, to be called the Jewish Company would become the economic arm of the movement. By unanimous vote, the delegates elected Theodore Herzl as president of the newborn Zionist Organization. Herzl recorded in his diary:

> If I were to sum up the Basle Congress in a single phrase . . . I would say: In Basle I created the Jewish State. Were I to say this aloud I would be greeted by universal laughter. But perhaps five years hence, in any case, certainly fifty years hence, everyone will perceive it.[25]

From the beginning of his efforts, Herzl had tried to open talks with the Ottoman Empire (centered in present-day Turkey), which ruled Palestine. The Ottoman Turks were not eager to speak with this polished, European Jew. Herzl did not obtain an audience with Sultan Abdul Hamid until the spring of 1901. By that time, the aging empire was in financial trouble, and Abdul Hamid himself was less than impressive, as Herzl described in his diary:

> I still see him before me, this Sultan of a dying robber empire. Small, shabby, with a badly dyed beard . . . long yellow teeth with a large gap in the right upper jaw, the fez pulled down over his head—which is probably bald—the protruding ears. . . . I see the enfeebled hands in the loose gloves, and the big, ill-fitting shirt cuffs. The bleeting voice . . . the timidity in every glance. And that apparition rules![26]

That apparition, that ghost of a man, would consider granting Palestinian territory to the Jews in return for their help with the Ottoman national debt. Herzl left in high spirits, certain that he could raise 2 million pounds to get the project started.

He was wrong. The wealthy Jewish bankers did not have the slightest interest in underwriting Hamid's regime. Even worse, many of Herzl's own colleagues were less than impressed by the sultan's assurances. The money was nowhere to be found, and the plan soon fell apart.

Herzl was willing to consider other places, South America, perhaps, or Africa. To him, the homeland did not have to be in Palestine. To Ahad Ha'am and the cultural Zionists, no other place would do. Herzl's priorities were all wrong, they said. He was so intent on political solutions to Jewish oppression, his critics claimed, that he ignored a rich spiritual and cultural heritage. Jews did not simply need a homeland, said Ahad Ha'am; they needed a *Jewish* homeland, where they could build a future on the foundation of their past. They needed Palestine.

## The Basle Program

*As restated in Alex Bein's biography of Theodore Herzl, the First Zionist Congress produced a clear, four-step program to implement its goals:*

"1) The programmatic encouragement of the settlement of Palestine with Jewish agricultural workers, laborers and artisans;

2) The unification and organization of all Jewry into local and general groups in accordance with the laws of their respective countries;

3) The strengthening of Jewish self-awareness and national consciousness (*Volksbewusstsein*);

4) The preparation of activity for the obtaining of the consent of the various governments, necessary for the fulfillment of the aim of Zionism."

*Sultan Abdul Hamid of the Ottoman Empire, which controlled Palestine, agreed to consider granting territory for a Jewish homeland in exchange for funds to relieve his empire's debt.*

Russian Jews listened to what Ahad Ha'am had to say. Theodore Herzl may have captured their imagination with his elegant Western ways, but it was Ahad Ha'am who captured their hearts. For these deeply observant people who had sacrificed so much for their faith, only one homeland would do: Palestine.

Herzl understood this. Although he was personally willing to consider other sites, he bowed to the will of the people. He had just turned down a British offer of territory in East Africa when tragedy struck the Jews of the Pale.

## Kishinev Massacre

The tragedy began in April 1903, soon after Czar Nicholas II succeeded to the throne. This weak, superstitious man was to be the last czar of imperial Russia. To counteract the social and political unrest abroad in the land, he needed a scapegoat, and he chose the Jews. The czar's hatred filtered down through the people. Soon, Jews faced renewed violence from their Christian neighbors.

Just before Easter, the city of Kishinev buzzed with a horrifying rumor: Jews had killed a young Christian man for their Passover ritual. The leaders of the Jewish community tried to counteract the rumor but to no avail. Beginning on Easter Sunday, mobs of enraged Christians raced through the Jewish section of the city, burning, looting, maiming, and killing. In three days of violence, mobs killed forty-five Jews, wounded eighty-six, and destroyed over fifteen hundred Jewish homes and shops.

*Anti-Semitism in Russia was carried to deadly extremes during the rule of Nicholas II.*

From the dark lessons of history, Herzl realized that Kishinev was just the beginning. The more unstable the government became, the more the people would blame some kind of "Jewish plot" for their misfortunes. To forestall a disaster, Herzl decided to reconsider British East Africa.

## The Uganda Proposal

The territory was in Kenya, but British colonial secretary Joseph Chamberlain called it "Uganda," and the name stuck. By any name, Herzl began to see it as a refuge for endangered Jews. Herzl quickly notified the colonial secretary of his interest. Through the British Zionist Leopold Greenberg, he commissioned a prominent law firm to prepare a charter, detailing the terms under which Jews would take possession of the land and build their colony.

Only then did he discuss the matter with the Zionist leadership. Longtime ally Max Nordau was less than enthusiastic about the whole scheme; it was not what the people wanted, he maintained. Herzl reassured him that Uganda was not intended to be a permanent answer to the "Jewish question." The colony would be a safe haven for persecuted Jews and a training ground for the true objective: Palestine.

On this basis, Nordau joined Herzl in presenting the plan to the membership. Herzl moved quickly once he made up his mind. At previous congresses, a map of Palestine had been prominently displayed on the dais (platform). When the delegates convened for the Sixth Zionist Congress on August 22, 1903, they were stunned to see a map of East Africa in its place. "Zion this certainly is not," Herzl

*Theodore Herzl proposed East Africa as a site for the future Jewish nation, but many Zionists vehemently favored Palestine.*

told them, "and can never become. . . . It is . . . an emergency measure which is intended . . . to prevent the loss of these detached remnants of our people."[27]

Nothing could have prepared Herzl for the reaction to this seemingly sensible proposal. Amid shouting, name-calling, and even tears, the delegates tried to come to terms with the issue. A motion to send a single investigative commission to East Africa squeaked by 295 to 177, with 100 abstentions. Chaim Weizmann biographer Norman Rose gives slightly different figures (292 for, 176 against, 143 abstaining). Regardless of the exact vote, the result was still the same: a break in the ranks that threatened the very existence of the Zionist Organization. As Rose stated:

> Formal parliamentary majorities were no longer sufficient—passions ran too high. The map of East Africa was torn down from the wall behind the speaker's dais. The Russian delegation filed out to consider their position in closed session. Some delegates sat down on the floor and observed the traditional, ritual mourning for the dead. One man fainted; others wept. When Herzl tried to pacify them, he was met with a shout of "traitor."[28]

Chaim Weizmann, the young Russian Zionist who once hailed Herzl as a "historic personality," became a leader of the opposition. After the Uganda proposal, Weizmann wrote:

> Herzl is not a nationalist, but a promoter of projects. He only takes external conditions into account, whereas the power on which we rely is the psychology of the people and its living desires.[29]

## Setting Sights on Zion

For all the controversy it triggered, the Uganda proposal did have positive consequences. It proved that only Palestine would be acceptable to the Zionists, and it indicated British sympathy for Jewish nationalism. That last fact was not lost on Chaim Weizmann, who was fast becoming a skilled politician and negotiator. "If the British government and people are what I think they are," he said at the time, "they will make us a better offer."[30] Those would be prophetic words.

The controversy over the Uganda proposal stretched beyond the Sixth Congress, spreading hard feelings and dissension throughout the movement. The British had problems from East Africans who did not want to hand over the territory to a foreign power. The British cooled to the idea, without officially retracting it. At the Seventh Congress in 1905, the Zionists who had supported the Uganda proposal formally withdrew their consideration and reaffirmed their commitment to Palestine.

By that time, Theodore Herzl had been dead for more than a year. He succumbed to heart failure and pneumonia on July 3, 1904, at the age of forty-four. Even people who had opposed his programs rushed to honor his memory. Theodore Herzl would always be remembered as the man who had united Jews throughout the world into a *people* again, a nation with leaders, functioning through the Zionist Organization. Neither ideological quarrels nor ruffled feelings could weaken his standing among the Jewish people.

Lithuanian-born David Wolffsohn became the second president of the Zionist Organization. Wolffsohn seemed the perfect choice to lead a divided movement. As the son of an eastern European rabbi, he understood the practical-minded Zionists of the Pale, their desire to colonize Palestine, and build the Yishuv. As a politically trained Zionist who learned from Herzl, he also knew that a nation could not exist without political autonomy and a land of its own.

Under Wolffsohn's leadership, the Zionist Organization became a nuts-and-bolts operation, founding settlements in Palestine, raising funds among the diaspora Jews, and supporting various cultural and educational projects.

At the Tenth Zionist Congress in 1911, Wolffsohn was replaced by an executive committee, whose function was to oversee the many development projects of the organization. At that same congress, the membership authorized extensive land purchases and recognized Hebrew as the official language of Zionism.

## More Divisions Within Zion

As the population of the Yishuv community grew and the Zionist program captured the imaginations of Jews everywhere, divisions continued to appear. Two of the most important were Mizrachi, the religious party; and Poalei Zion (the labor Zionist party), which combined the principles of socialism with the spirit of Zionism.

Mizrachi was originally founded in 1893 by Rabbi Samuel Mohilever, a student of Talmud (a vast body of postbiblical Jewish religious writings) and a devout Orthodox Jew. Mohilever well knew that Herzl and most of the rest of the leadership were intent on setting a secular course for the new nation. He hoped to make the Mizrachi society into a living reminder of the need for religious observance in a truly Jewish state.

In 1902, Rabbi Isaac Jacob Reines almost single-handedly transformed Mizrachi into a political force for religious orthodoxy in the Yishuv. Though always a minority, Mizrachi opened the door of Zionism to devout Jews who would otherwise find no place within the movement.

Poalei Zion was a political organization that combined Zionism and Marxist socialism. From Zionism, they took the dedication to their ancestral homeland. From socialism, they took the glorification of physical labor and the idea of public ownership of all property. From this fusion of

### The Spirit of the Chalutzim

*In 1907, a schoolteacher named Yosef Vitkin issued a ringing call to Jewish youth. His words are quoted in Howard M. Sachar's* A History of Israel.

"The major causes of our blundering [as pioneers] are our search for a shortcut, and our belief that the attainment of our goal is close at hand. Out of this belief we have built castles in the air . . . and have turned aside with contempt from the longer and harder road, which is perhaps the surest, and in the end, the shortest. . . . Awake, O youth of Israel! Come to the aid of your people. Your people lies in agony. Rush to its side. Band together; discipline yourselves for life or death; forget all the precious bonds of your childhood; leave them behind forever without a shadow of regret, and answer the call of your people."

*Pioneers of an early twentieth-century kibbutz in Palestine take a break from their labor. Kibbutzim were communities in which members lived and worked as part of a collective.*

two revolutionary movements came the heroic figure of the *chalutz* (pioneer). During the second migration, or aliyah (1904–1914), sixty thousand of these idealistic chalutzim went to Palestine to put their social ideals to the test. With socialist zeal and youthful chutzpah (colossal nerve), they meant to create a new Yishuv, built, governed, and protected by Jews.

## A Generation of Builders

In Russia and eastern Europe, Jews had never been known as laborers, and certainly not as farmers. They were tailors and tradesmen, merchants and lenders, scholars and teachers and dealers in ideas. Most immigrants of the first aliyah had maintained that occupational pattern. Those who did own land were not farmers but agricultural employers. They hired Arab peasants to do the actual work.

One of the first objectives of the chalutzim was to create a strong Jewish working class that would become the heart, muscle, and nerve of a "reborn" Jewish community. To build a socialist foundation for that society following the principles of Poalei Zion, they established labor exchanges, community kitchens, medical clinics, and other social services. They formed agricultural settlements where members lived together as equals, sharing the work and the rewards.

Some of these communities were cooperatives called moshavim (singular, moshav), in which families owned their homes and land, but the business of farming was a community enterprise. Other communities were true collectives called kibbutzim (singular, kibbutz). Individual kibbutzniks (members of kibbutzim) had no private property: not the land they farmed, the houses they lived in, nor even the clothes they wore.

Nation-building went beyond the creation of new political and social institutions, extending even to language. For hundreds of years, Jews had spoken the languages of their diaspora homelands. The closest

## A Summons to Arabs

*This summons from an anonymous anti-Zionist to the Arabs of Palestine in July 1914 is quoted in Mark Tessler's* A History of the Israeli-Palestinian Conflict.

"Countrymen! We summon you in the name of the country which is in mourning, in the name of the homeland which is lamenting, in the name of Arabia, in the name of Syria, in the name of our country, Palestine, whose lot is evil, in the name of everything that is dear to you. . . . Men! Do you want to be slaves and servants to people who are notorious in the world and in history? Do you wish to be slaves to the Zionists who have come to you to expel you from your country, saying that this country is theirs?"

thing to a Jewish language was Yiddish, a blend of medieval German and Hebrew, with phrases borrowed from Russian, Polish, and other sources. To the young firebrands of the second aliyah, Yiddish was a language of oppression, born in the ghetto.

They looked to the work of Eliezer Ben Yehuda (1858–1922), a linguist who transformed Hebrew from a dead liturgical (religious ritual) language into a living, breathing means of communication. Along with draining swamps, irrigating deserts, and building villages, the chalutzim set themselves the task of learning Hebrew. These efforts began a long struggle to transform an accidental collection of Jewish strangers into a nation with an identity of its own.

## The Fortunes of War

World War I was a turning point for the infant Yishuv. This "war to end all wars," as U.S. president Woodrow Wilson called it, pitted the Allies (England, France, the United States, and for a time, Russia) against the Central Powers (Germany, Austria-Hungary, the Ottoman Empire). As a possession of the Ottoman Empire, Palestine suffered greatly during the war. Both Arab nationalists and Zionists resisted the presence of troops in their homeland. Mark Tessler wrote:

The [Ottoman troops] arrested both Arab nationalists and Zionist leaders, executing some of the former and giving most of the latter a choice between prision and exile. As a result, overt Arab nationalist activity in Palestine ceased and Zionist activists . . . went into exile. The general population suffered as well. Food was in short supply . . . partly because of the . . . Ottoman army, which used Palestine as a base for the fighting in Sinai [the southern desert region]. Crops and livestock were commandeered for the troops, and trees were cut down to be used as fuel. Also, tens of thousands of Arab peasants were conscripted [drafted into the army], adding to the dislocation and contributing further to a decline in agricultural producion.[31]

This kind of conduct did not endear the Ottoman Empire to the people of Palestine, a fact the British used to make alliances with both Arabs and Jews. On October 24, 1915, Sir Henry McMahon won over the Arabs with a formal agreement to support their emancipation in Palestine.

On November 2, 1917, British diplomat Sir Arthur Balfour made a similar promise to the Jews. The Balfour Declaration, as it came to be known, was in the form of a letter from Lord Balfour to Baron Edmond de Rothschild, unofficial leader of British Jewry. In language that Zionists hailed as "the Magna Carta of Jewish liberties,"[32] the declaration called for "the establishment in Palestine of a national home for the Jewish people."[33]

On November 11, 1918, World War I ended in victory for the Allies. The Ottoman Empire crumbled, Germany staggered under a war debt imposed by a punitive treaty, and Britain took over the administration of Palestine under a mandate (authorization to govern) from the League of Nations. Both Arabs and Jews expected the British to make good on their wartime promises. Those expectations would not be fulfilled, nor would the hopes of war-weary nations trying to make sense of mass confusion. While ending the First World War, humankind was already sowing the seeds of the Second.

# 4 Between Two Wars

Under the British mandate, the Zionist Organization in Palestine became the Jewish Agency, the official representative of the Yishuv. In time, it would become the shadow government of a nation that did not yet exist. In the aftermath of a divisive war, the agency had little time for political considerations. The entire Yishuv struggled to absorb a third aliyah (1919–1923), composed mainly of labor Zionists from Russia and Poland, and then a fourth (1924–1931), which brought refugees from the cities of eastern Europe to the cities of Palestine.

## Marching to Zion

The third aliyah was made of idealistic young people who dreamed of building a nation with their own hands. They were well prepared for the task, thanks to the work of kibbutznik Joseph Trumpeldor and a project that began as an accident. As a captain in the British military, Trumpeldor had commanded the Zion Mule Corps, a daring transport unit that kept Allied supply lines open during the Dardanelles campaign of 1915.

After completing that mission, he went to Russia to recruit a Jewish legion to fight for the liberation of Palestine. His timing for this project was unfortunate: he arrived in 1917, when the Communist revolution was tearing the country apart and Russia had resigned from the Allied forces. The hard-pressed government banned recruiting, so Trumpeldor decided that if he could not take Jewish warriors to Palestine, he would send Jewish pioneers.

He traveled through the Pale, forming Hehalutz (the pioneer) youth groups and establishing training centers where would-be farmers could learn the fundamentals of agriculture and prepare themselves mentally and physically for life in Palestine. Interest in Hehalutz quickly spread into Poland, Lithuania, and Romania, and what was then Czechoslovakia.

According to historian Celia S. Heller, Hehalutz youngsters

> became imbued with the idea of the regeneration of the Jewish people in their ancient homeland. Numerous cultural activities of the Zionist youth organizations revolved around this goal, the study of Hebrew being among the foremost. Small study groups met periodically, under the guidance of a senior member to discuss ideological and social issues.[34]

This intense preparation paid off. Golda Meir, future prime minister of Israel

## Zionist Youth Groups

*Young Jews found refuge and hope in a variety of Zionist organizations, from the radically socialist Hashomer Hatzair to the right-wing Betar. The following two testimonials are quoted in Celia S. Heller's* On the Edge of Destruction.

"[Hashomer Hatzair,] which I joined early . . . had a decisive effect on my life. The older members succeeded in binding us so to the organization that it became precious to us. There was not a day when I did not spend a few hours there. Our guides organized lectures and discussions on varied subjects and instilled a way of independent thinking and healthy criticism."

Said a member of the rival Betar: "Socialism in theory had no value for me. . . . I became convinced that socialism would not solve the Jewish problem, a solution for which I longed and continue longing. I joined the opposition; the Revisionist Party, the Betar, to work for the good of our people, for the creation of a Jewish state."

and a member of the third aliyah, once described her immigrant group as

> girls and boys in their teens. They had nobody to care for, they carried no responsibility for anybody except themselves, most of them burned their bridges saying, "This is it. There is no going back." They came mostly from Eastern Europe, really with an enthusiasm, on a mission, a historic mission, although they never said it. And they had no complaints.[35]

Meir herself came from the United States, one of a group who responded to speaking and fund-raising tours by Zionists from Palestine. Many American Jews were dedicated to Zionist principles but did not necessarily plan to emigrate. They supported the movement with financial contributions and political activity on behalf of the Jewish state. Meir's group considered it their duty to make aliyah and personally join in the work of building the Yishuv.

## The Beginnings of Conflict

The Zionists were so intent upon their own program that they failed to notice Arab reactions to their presence. Each influx of Jewish immigrants, each new building project or Zionist organization had an impact on the Arab community, and that impact was often negative. The British were also becoming concerned. Their mandate required them to administer Palestine for all its inhabitants and to keep the peace. Anything that endangered that peace appeared to them as a threat.

When Zionists bought land from wealthy absentee owners, Arab tenant farmers lost their homes and fields. When

## Justice Brandeis on the Zionist Pioneers

*Louis D. Brandeis (1856–1941), first Jew appointed to the U.S. Supreme Court, wrote movingly on the Zionist pioneers in his 1915 essay, "Our Jewish Pilgrim Fathers," here excerpted from* Zionism: A Basic Reader.

"To the worldly wise these efforts at colonization appeared very foolish. Nature and man presented obstacles in Palestine which appeared almost insuperable [not to be overcome]; and the colonists were in fact ill-equipped for their task, save their spirit of devotion and self-sacrifice. The land, harassed by centuries of misrule, was treeless and apparently sterile, and it was infested with malaria. The Government offered them no security, either as to life or property. The colonists themselves were not only unfamiliar with the character of the country, but

*U.S. Supreme Court Justice Louis D. Brandeis.*

were ignorant of the farmer's life which they proposed to lead. . . . [W]ithin a generation these Jewish Pilgrim Fathers, and those who followed them, have succeeded in establishing these two fundamental propositions:

*First:* That Palestine is fit for the modern Jew.

*Second:* That the modern Jew is fit for Palestine.

Over forty self-governing Jewish colonies attested to this remarkable achievement."

---

Zionists demanded Jews-only hiring policies in the fields and factories, Arab laborers lost their jobs. When Zionists cultivated the desert, the nomadic Bedouin lost the freedom to roam. When Zionists demanded a Jewish state, middle- and upper-class Arabs feared for their future under a new government that did not understand their religious and cultural values.

Even without a recognized government, the Jews were providing themselves with the trappings of nationhood. Labor Zionists in 1920 founded a Jews-only labor federation called Histadrut, which eventually provided a full range of social services to Jewish workers, including medical care and housing. Histadrut also created jobs through its Public Works Office and a semi-independent economic development corporation called Chevrat Ovdim (the Workers' Association). The Public Works Office built factories, roads, quarries, and homes. Chevrat Ovdim established a marketing cooperative for kibbutz dairy products, nonprofit housing complexes for workers, even an insurance company. All of these enterprises created jobs for Jews but not for Arabs.

In April 1920, three days of Arab riots in Jerusalem left five Jews and four Arabs dead, and more than two hundred injured. Vladimir Jabotinsky, a militant Zionist who longed to resurrect the ancient image of the fighting Jew, organized a makeshift defense force to protect Jewish life and property. After a few skirmishes, the British

*Vladimir Jabotinsky founded Haganah, the secret Zionist militia, to defend the Jewish settlement in Palestine.*

authorities quashed the fighting and sent Jabotinsky to jail for "inciting violence." He was later granted amnesty and released.

The fighting group Jabotinsky organized grew into a secret Zionist militia known simply as Haganah (defense). Haganah bases were often located on isolated kibbutzim. There the fighters protected the community, guarded the fields, and trained for the struggle that lay ahead.

The rift between Arabs and Jews continued to widen, leaving the British struggling with the demands of two rival cultures, each convinced that the other endangered its very existence. Under these conditions, the fourth aliyah began in 1924. It brought a group of middle-class businesspeople fleeing anti-Jewish economic policies in Poland. Under Polish finance minister Wladyslaw Grabski, one-third of the Jewish-owned businesses went bankrupt, and thousands of employed Jews lost their jobs to gentiles.

Fourth aliyah immigrants had little interest in farming; they settled in the cities where they could re-create the lives they left behind. Merchants opened stores, tradesmen opened workshops, industrialists opened manufacturing facilities. Construction became the largest industry in the Yishuv, as Jerusalem and Haifa doubled in size and Tel Aviv grew from a sleepy suburb into the first modern, all-Jewish city in Palestine. Altogether, the fourth aliyah added seventy-five thousand people to the Jewish community.

## Choosing Directions

The period of the fourth aliyah was marked by profound changes to the Zionist movement, the Yishuv, and the status of the European diaspora. With the death of Max Nordau in 1924, the last link to the Herzl era was gone. So was the belief that one grand, diplomatic stroke could call a Jewish nation into being.

Chaim Weizmann became president of the World Zionist Organization in 1920. As a son of poverty and the Pale he had lower expectations. According to Weizmann biographer Norman Rose,

> Weizmann rejected the narrow conception of the Herzlians and defined political Zionism in the broadest possible sense. For him, practical work in Palestine would be the lever to pry a Charter [recognizing a Jewish state] out of . . . foreign governments. One was dependent on the other. The achievements, sacrifices, and experiences of the Yishuv—a slow and grad-

*Chaim Weizmann rose from the poverty and oppression of the Russian Pale to become president of the World Zionist Organization in 1920.*

ual process—would provide [a case] for political power.[36]

Weizmann drew criticism for that "slow and gradual process." He was too prone to compromise, critics said, too eager to please the British and placate the Arabs. Ever the wily old statesman, Weizmann listened to opposing viewpoints, but when the talking was over he stood his ground:

> There is no royal road to Palestine. Often we shall conquer, often we shall sustain defeat. We will build stone by stone in Palestine till the time comes when once more a tribunal will sit before which we will be able to formulate demands. . . . Then your future leader will appear before this tribunal and you will be able to rely on work accomplished, small perhaps, but healthy, and honest, and genuine. For this time you must wait with patience and courage as becomes an ancient race. . . . Do not clamour for . . . successes that . . . will afterward turn back upon your work. I can only proceed along this road, for it is bound up in my faith and in my experience. If you want a quicker route, then you will have to choose another leader.[37]

True to his broad vision of what a Jewish state ought to be, Weizmann devoted substantial time and effort to establishing a Hebrew university in Jerusalem. On April 1, 1925, the university was officially opened with a dedication ceremony that included Lord Balfour, dressed in formal academic robes as chancellor of Cambridge University. For Chaim Weizmann, the ceremony was the fulfillment of a dream that had started in 1901.

For Vladimir Jabotinsky, it was a sign of everything that had gone wrong with

*Lord Balfour speaks at the dedication of the Hebrew university in Jerusalem on April 1, 1925. Establishing the university was an important goal for Chaim Weizmann.*

Zionism. Weizmann's group seemed content with a few thousand immigrants here, a handful of kibbutzim there, and a Hebrew university thrown in for good measure. Jabotinsky wanted more. Just days after the university dedication, he launched the Revisionist movement with a fiery speech, made not in Palestine to the chalutzim, but in Paris to members of the diaspora. Revisionists, he said, would settle for nothing less than an independent commonwealth, created and governed by a Jewish majority. Arab opposition was inevitable, he said, but the Jewish claim upon the ancestral homeland was absolute. There could be no compromise, even in the name of peace.

While Jabotinsky and Weizmann debated the future of Zionism, an Austrian-born extremist published his first book. He wrote it in 1924, in a German prison, where he was serving time for an attempted revolution that started in a Munich beer hall and ended in the city jail.

The book was *Mein Kampf* (*My Struggle*), a lengthy mishmash of theories, recollections, and prejudices. The author was Adolf Hitler. Within ten years, he would become Führer (absolute dictator) of the German nation and adopt an anti-Semitic platform bent on exterminating European Jewry.

Hitler's rise to power transformed the fifth and final aliyah (1933–1939) into a desperate scramble for escape. This exodus occurred just as the British had begun to rethink their commitment to a Jewish homeland in Palestine. Arab resistance was stronger and deeper than they had expected.

## More Violence

The British still remembered the Jewish High Holy Days of September 1928, when an apparently minor disagreement began yet another round of violence. A group of Orthodox Jews wanted to hold services at

## Smuggling Jews into Palestine

*Helping illegal immigrants during the mandate years not only required courage but inventiveness as well, as this story from Kibbutz Kfar Giladi demonstrates. Kibbutz member Rachel Yanait Ben-Zui narrates the story, which was taken from* A Treasury of Jewish Inspirational Stories.

"On one spring day in 1927, [kibbutznik Manya Shochat] was driving back to the *kibbutz* . . . [when she met] a *kibbutz* wagon filled with hay and driven by Dov Krol, then fourteen years old. They began talking when, suddenly, three men and a woman ran right up to them, looking wild and crazed. They collapsed as they reached Manya, begging her to hide them from the Arabs. . . . Manya wanted to help, but the area was completely open, with no place at all to hide. Manya turned to young Dov, who smiled and said he had an idea. He drove his mules to one side, steering quickly and forcing the wagon to turn over. All the hay fell out. The four immigrants lay down on the camp ground and were covered with the hay. Moments later eight Arab police arrived, asking Manya and Dov if they had seen four people. Dov . . . said he had seen four crazy-looking people running very fast toward [the town of] Jachula. The exhausted police lay down near the haystack to rest. Finally, they continued on their way. Dov looked around to make sure they had really gone and then put the people in his wagon. . . . They arrived back at Kfar Giladi within two hours."

the revered Western Wall, last remnant of the ancient Temple in Jerusalem. In keeping with their tradition, they put up a screen to separate male and female worshippers. The Muslims, who also revered the Temple, accused the Jews of illegally altering the site with their screen.

This complaint set in motion a series of charges and countercharges that lasted for nearly a year. Jews and Arabs disrupted one another's worship services at every possible opportunity. Finally, on August 24, 1929, crowds of armed Arabs pushed through the narrow, winding streets of the Old City and attacked the Orthodox Jewish quarter.

From there, they struck out to Hebron, Haifa, Jaffa, and Tel Aviv, attacking kibbutzim and other rural settlements along the way. The Jews fought back, determined to assert their rights in Palestine. By the time the British got the situation under control, 133 Jews and 87 Arabs were dead.

The Jews blamed the Arabs for starting the violence; the Arabs blamed the

Jews for pushing them too far. Caught between the two sides, the British mandate government ordered a complete investigation of the incident.

A commission headed by Sir Walter Shaw took five weeks to come to some startling conclusions: although the Arabs started the violence, the rapid growth of the Yishuv had triggered their anger. The mandate authority should therefore restrict Jewish immigration and land acquisition.

The Zionists were stunned: what about the promises of Balfour? Politics had undermined that historic declaration. A new leadership ruled in Britain, men who did not share their predecessors' commitment to Zionism. The Shaw Report had an immediate effect on British policy in Eretz Israel. On May 12, 1930, the government suspended thirty-three hundred Jewish immigration certificates. This was a sign of things to come.

## Aliyah of the Refugees

German Jews were different from others who sought refuge in the ancient homeland. They were called *yekkes* in Palestine, though nobody knows where the word came from, what it means, whether it should be considered an insult or a compliment.

Of the estimated seven hundred thousand Jews in Germany and Austria when Hitler became chancellor in 1933, between fifty thousand and sixty thousand sought refuge in Palestine. Distinguished Israeli journalist Tom Segev wrote:

> They came shocked and confused, having been uprooted from a country they had loved as their own. The awareness that they had erred in feeling at home, and the need to emigrate to a distant land, was a catastrophe for them—not an ascent, as in the literal sense of *aliyah* . . . but a descent.[38]

With this view of their situation, it is no wonder that many German Jews had a difficult time assimilating into the Yishuv. They were

> mocked for the values of formal education they brought with them, for their professional training, for their attention to the quality of their work. . . . Most German immigrants continued to speak German among themselves . . . and many discovered that they could get by without [speaking Hebrew]. Nothing more clearly brought home their foreignness and alienation than their inability—sometimes their refusal—to learn Hebrew. Nothing else put them in such deep and painful conflict with the Zionist ethos [values] of the yishuv.[39]

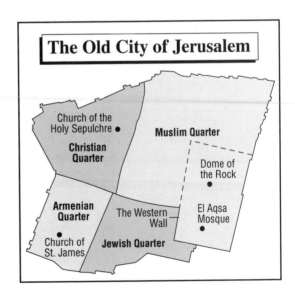

**The Old City of Jerusalem**

Church of the Holy Sepulchre •

**Christian Quarter**

**Muslim Quarter**

Dome of the Rock •

**Armenian Quarter**

The Western Wall

El Aqsa Mosque •

• Church of St. James

**Jewish Quarter**

To Zionists, speaking Hebrew was a sign of nationhood, as well as an unbreakable link with the Jewish past. Eliezer Ben-Yehuda, the linguist who resurrected Hebrew from the religious past, was held in the highest regard, a Zionist hero who was often mentioned in the same breath with Theodore Herzl.

Even as "outsiders," the German refugees contributed to the Yishuv. Like their predecessors in the fourth aliyah, they were drawn to urban centers rather than rural ones. As a group they were well educated, with many experienced physicians, attorneys, professors, and teachers in their ranks. Others had business and industrial backgrounds.

Between 1931 and 1935, German refugees swelled the population of Tel Aviv and Jaffa from 46,000 to 135,000. During the same period, the Jewish population of Jerusalem increased from 53,000 to 70,000.

## Growing Arab Resistance

As the Jewish population grew, Arab resistance stiffened. In the spring of 1936, rioting in the streets of Jaffa led to a bloody uprising, which quickly spread to the rest of Palestine. When Arab leaders called a general strike, Arab peasants in the countryside who had lost their farms because of Zionist land purchases joined with urban Arab workers who had lost their jobs to Jews-only hiring policies.

The strike lasted until October, throwing the economy into disarray and straining British resources to the breaking

*Thousands of German Jews fled to Palestine during the early 1930s when Hitler rose to power. Here, new arrivals check in at an immigrant camp.*

*Palmach (pictured) was established when Orden Wingate, a British captain, trained Haganah soldiers to become an elite commando unit.*

point. Bands of Arab rebels roamed the country, bombing police stations, sabotaging government installations, turning roads into deadly mine fields. Even when the strike ended, they kept fighting.

Neither the Zionists nor the British fully understood why. Arab objections to Jewish settlement went beyond economics and politics. Beneath these practical concerns there was a deeper, more emotional, reason: the Arabs felt threatened by Jewish social patterns.

Jewish farmers were not a true peasant class, bound to the land they worked. They were educated, politically aware, given to endless debates about ideologies. Arabs considered Jewish influence to be even more damaging in the cities. An unnamed Arab told journalist Carl Raswan,

> Money is God [in Tel Aviv]. [The city] is an ulcer eating into our own country. If it is what the Jews want to make of Palestine, I wish my children dead. We do not mind poverty, but we weep when our peace is taken away. We lived a modest and contented life, but what shall we do if our children grow up to ape the noisy ways of these new people?[40]

The hard-pressed British sent a commission to Palestine to examine and report on the situation. Under the chairmanship of Lord Robert Peel, one-time British secretary of state, the commission found that Britain had made conflicting promises to Arabs and Jews. The final report recommended dividing Palestine into separate Jewish and Arab states. A second commission, appointed to fix the borders for this partition, concluded instead that it would never work. Throughout this high-level tug-of-war, the unrest in Palestine continued to drain British resources.

Arab rebels seized control of territory outside the major cities, hoping to reclaim the countryside. The Jews fought back. Led by a brave and occasionally reckless commander named Yitzchak Sadeh, Haganah forces fought to protect Jewish life and property from Arab attack. Sadeh was a grizzled veteran of the Russian Army, a firm believer in the old truism that the best defense is a good offense. So was the British officer who took the Jewish cause as his own.

Captain Orden Wingate was a Christian Zionist who believed that restoring Jews to their homeland fulfilled biblical prophesy. He helped to transform Sadeh's inexperienced fighters into a commando squad that became the core of Palmach, an elite first-strike unit of Haganah.

## The White Paper

While the Jews, the Arabs, and the British fought it out in Palestine, Nazi aggression pushed Europe to the brink of war. The Germans annexed Austria in March 1938 and invaded Czechoslovakia in March 1939. Nobody tried to stop them.

Jews fleeing the Nazi onslaught flooded into Palestine. When the Arabs threatened to join with Germany if this immigration did not stop, the British government issued the notorious White Paper (an official policy statement) of May 17, 1939. This document renounced the Balfour Declaration by stating that partition was "impractical" and by placing new restrictions on Jewish immigration and land purchases.

However serious the situation was in Palestine, it took a backseat to increasing concerns over Nazi aggression in Europe. On September 1, 1939, Germany invaded Poland. This time, Britain and her allies responded in force: World War II had begun. It pitted the Allied powers (Great Britain, the Soviet Union, and the United States) against the Axis powers (Germany, Italy, and Japan).

The Jews of Palestine faced a devil's choice between opposing the White Paper and fighting the Nazis. David Ben-Gurion, chairman of the Jewish Agency and therefore unofficial "prime minister" of the Yishuv, put the dilemma into perspective with one sentence: "We shall fight the war against Hitler as if there were no White Paper, and we shall fight the White Paper as if there were no war."[41] As a matter of policy, this compromise left much to be desired; as a practical measure, it was perhaps the only way to preserve the Yishuv.

# 5 No Man's Land

World War II forever redefined Jewish history. The ancient Jews had been conquered many times, enslaved, dispersed, and persecuted. For generations, they had lived as a despised minority in the diaspora. None of that had prepared them for the Nazi death machine, an entire bureaucracy dedicated to the systematic murder of Jews.

## The Yishuv in Wartime

In his book *The Seventh Million: The Israelis and the Holocaust*, Tom Segev describes the position of the Yishuv leadership as "essentially one of helplessness. They rescued a few thousand Jews from Europe. They could, perhaps, have saved more, but they could not save millions."[42]

The leadership of the Jewish Agency understood this hard fact all too well. Early in the war, David Ben-Gurion, president of the Jewish Agency, made it clear that protecting the Yishuv was the agency's top priority, not rescuing European Jewry. His reasoning was straightforward and blunt: the Yishuv was a frontier society surrounded by hostile forces. That society needed workers, fighters, and builders who could transform a wasteland into a homeland. Since saving everyone was impossible, rescuers could not avoid making a choice. Why not choose people who would become assets to the Yishuv?

The First World War had freed Palestine from Ottoman rule and produced the Balfour Declaration. Ben-Gurion was determined that the Second World War would produce a Jewish state. He geared everything to that aim, and for the most part, the Yishuv went along with him.

European Jews faced a choice of their own: stay in their homes and hope the danger would pass or escape to a place of safety. Both choices were dangerous, and both produced their share of senseless tragedies.

## The *Patria*

The fate of the *Patria*, a commandeered ocean liner that had seen better days, provoked grief and outrage from Jews all over the world. In the winter of 1940, two battered ships bearing nearly two thousand Romanian Jews put in to Haifa bay. Acting under authority of the mandatory government, British patrol boats refused them permission to go ashore.

The dazed passengers from both ships were transferred to the larger *Patria* for transport to a holding facility on the island

## The Challenge of Survival

*On April 17, 1938, Albert Einstein spoke before the National Labor Committee for Palestine, reflecting on the mounting threat in Europe and the challenge in Palestine. His words were included in his book* Ideas and Opinions.

"Rarely since the Conquest of Jerusalem by Titus has the Jewish community experienced a period of greater oppression than prevails at the present time. In some respects, indeed, our own time is even more troubled, for man's possibilities of emigration are more limited today than they were then.

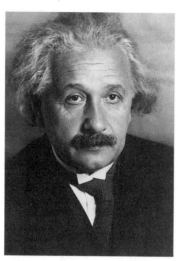

*Albert Einstein*

Yet we shall survive this period, too, no matter how much sorrow, no matter how heavy a loss in life it may bring. A community like ours, which is a community purely by reason of tradition, can only be strengthened by pressure from without. For today every Jew feels that to be a Jew means to bear a serious responsibility not only to his own community, but also toward humanity."

of Mauritius in the Indian Ocean. The plight of these refugees engaged sympathy all over the world. Jews in the Yishuv protested with a general strike. In London, Zionists begged the government to overrule the mandatory authority in this case.

The British said no, the Romanian Jews remained prisoners aboard the *Patria,* and the Haganah decided to take matters into its own hands. Agents slipped aboard the ship under cover of darkness and placed homemade bombs in the engine compartment. The plan was simple: blow up the engines so the ship could not sail. Faced with such an impasse, the British might relent and allow the refugees into the country. At the least, disabling the ship would buy some time.

In carrying out the plan, the Haganah agents miscalculated the amount of explosive needed to do the job. The explosion that was supposed to cripple *Patria*'s engines ripped through the hull, sinking the ship in a matter of minutes. Nearly three hundred people died while their comrades watched in helpless horror.

The *Patria* was not the last of the ill-fated refugee ships. The British continued to enforce the ban on immigration, and the Jews continued to defy it, as Norman Rose wrote:

> No administrative statute could prevent the boats from running the British blockade. *Patria, Darien, Struma, Mekfure, Nyasa, Salvador, Exodus*—names of vessels engraved on the Jewish conscience as bearing martyrs to the Jewish state. The sinkings, the drownings, the internments, the expulsions served as a permanent reminder to Zionist leaders that after the war a political solution would have to be found for the survivors.[43]

## Fighting the Good Fight

True to Ben-Gurion's promise, the Yishuv walked a thin line between opposing the White Paper in Palestine and supporting the Allied war effort in Europe. In general, this meant reducing attacks against the mandatory government. Even the extremists supported Britain's fight against Nazi Germany.

The leadership of the Yishuv offered to form a semi-independent Jewish force to protect the Middle East against a Nazi invasion, as described by Mark Tessler.

> This Jewish army was to have its own flag and to be led by Jewish junior officers, although it would fight within the structure of the British military and be under the general command of senior British officers.[44]

The Jewish Agency pushed hard for such a unit, but the British resisted. A Jewish force fighting under its own flag sounded too much like an army defending a sovereign nation. Arab reaction to that would be swift and quite probably violent.

In 1942 the British sent fifteen hundred Palmach commandos on a special mission in the Libyan desert, but on the question of a real "Jewish army," they continued to stall. Not until the war was nearly over in the autumn of 1944 would they send a Jewish brigade into action.

## The Biltmore Program

In the spring of 1942, Jewish life in Palestine still centered around preserving and building the Yishuv. At a conference held in New York City's Biltmore Hotel, nearly seven hundred Zionists gathered to formulate a new and more ambitious plan for the Jewish state.

Jews worldwide felt the pressure to unite Zionist factions behind a policy they could all affirm. There was no more time for infighting. Reports from Nazi-occupied Europe spoke of ghettos and death camps, of Jews enslaved and murdered. In New York City, even the most idealistic delegates stopped talking about building a Jewish utopia and concentrated on the desperate need to create a place of refuge for European Jews.

The Biltmore Program, as it came to be called, did not juggle borders for some new partition scheme, nor make concessions to the despised White Paper. The program called for all of Palestine to be immediately given over to the Jews:

> The Conference urges that the gates of Palestine be opened; that the Jewish

Agency be vested with control of immigration into Palestine and with the necessary authority for upbuilding the country, including the development of its unoccupied and uncultivated lands; and that Palestine be established as a Jewish Commonwealth integrated into the structure of the new democratic world. Then and only then will the age-old wrong to the Jewish people be righted.[45]

## Policies, Politics, and Personality

In a sense, the Biltmore Program did unite squabbling Zionist factions behind a common goal. Unfortunately, it did not unite them on the question of how to reach that goal. Methods became an ongoing contro-versy between the old order, represented by Chaim Weizmann, president of the Zionist Organization, and the new order of David Ben-Gurion of the Jewish Agency.

The dispute between the two men was as much a matter of personal style as conflicting philosophy. In dealing with the mandatory government, Weizmann was willing to negotiate; Ben-Gurion was ready to fight. Each believed the methods of the other would frustrate the Zionist cause. The two would clash throughout the war. Immediately after the Biltmore conference, Ben-Gurion denounced Weizmann as an autocrat and a bungler, with a "fossilized" approach to politics.

In their public debates, Weizmann usually got the upper hand. His was the more reasoned approach, and he had learned from experience how to appear statesman-like and controlled. In private, though, he sometimes had emotional outbursts. The

### The Killing Squads

*In 1942, a report smuggled out of Warsaw documented the horrors of the* Einsatzkommandos, *the Nazi death squads. The report is recorded in Christopher Simpson's* The Splendid Blond Beast.

"From the day the Russo-German war broke out, the Germans embarked on the physical extermination of the Jewish population on Polish soil. . . . It began . . . in the summer months of 1941. The following system was applied everywhere: men, fourteen to sixty years old, were driven to a single place—a square or a cemetery, where they were slaughtered, or shot by machine-guns, or killed by hand grenades. They had to dig their own graves. Children in orphanages, inmates in old-age homes, [the] sick in hospitals were shot, women were killed on the streets. In many towns Jews were carried off to an 'unknown destination' and killed in the adjacent woods."

*David Ben-Gurion (bottom row, center) and Chaim Weizmann frequently butted heads over political methods. Ben-Gurion criticized Weizmann as being autocratic and outdated.*

following letter was written and rewritten, but never mailed:

> I have watched Mr. Ben Gurion carefully during his stay here [in New York City]. His conduct and deportment were painfully reminiscent of the petty dictator, a type one meets with so often in public life now. They are all shaped on a definite pattern: they are humorless, thin-lipped, morally stunted, fanatical and stubborn, apparently frustrated in some ambition.[46]

The posturing between Weizmann and Ben-Gurion changed nothing, least of all the British determination to enforce the provisions of the 1939 White Paper. The vast majority of Zionists continued to support the Biltmore Program, with its claim to all of Palestine.

As to method, Vladimir Jabotinsky's Revisionists became involved. Jabotinsky himself died in 1940, but his organization had produced Irgun Zvai Leumi (National Military Organization, called "Etzel" for its He-brew initials, or simply "Irgun"), and its even more extremist offshoot, Lehi (Hebrew acronym for Lohamei Herut Yisrael or Fighters for Israel's Freedom). After the Biltmore conference, they stepped up attacks on Arab and British positions in Palestine. Whatever the cost, these militants meant to transform Palestine into the sanctuary the Jewish people desperately needed.

In the summer of 1942, "desperate" may have seemed like an overstatement, but in December the Allies issued a chilling statement concerning the fate of Jews under Nazi rule:

> From all the [Nazi-] occupied countries Jews are being transported, in conditions of appalling horror and brutality, to Eastern Europe. . . . None of those taken away are ever heard from again. The able-bodied are slowly worked to death in labor camps. The infirm are left to die of exposure and starvation or are deliberately massacred in mass executions. The number

*The emaciated bodies of Holocaust victims are grim evidence of the atrocities committed by the Nazi government. The early reports of the Nazis' treatment of Jews were difficult for many people to believe.*

of victims of these bloody cruelties is reckoned in many hundreds of thousands of entirely innocent men, women and children.[47]

Many people simply refused to believe such reports; that kind of brutality was unthinkable, even for Nazis. Perhaps the sources overstated the danger. Perhaps frightened people assumed the worst when they lost contact with loved ones who had been taken by the Nazis.

## Heroes of the Yishuv

These reports of mass murder had shaken the Yishuv to its very foundations. The Jewish Agency began to look for ways to help

the unfortunate people trapped under Nazi control. In 1943, someone suggested an idea that was more daring than sensible: to recruit Palestinian Jews who were natives of Balkan countries, train them as paratroopers, and drop them behind enemy lines to conduct rescue and resistance operations. They could also gather vital intelligence information for the Allies.

Nearly two hundred volunteered for the mission, mostly young kibbutzniks who were no strangers to hard, physically demanding work. Thirty were chosen. They would return to the countries of their birth to give help and hope to Jews who were trapped there. They went through an intensive training program, first with the Palmach in commando tactics and survival skills, and then with the British in parachute jumping and Morse code.

According to Peter Hay, biographer of paratrooper Chana Szenes, Zionist ideology was also part of the training:

Her first seminars were not military but ideological. . . . The classes were designed to orient and even indoctrinate volunteers about Jewish ideals and values. . . . The Jewish Agency and the Haganah considered it of the highest propaganda value that anybody representing Eretz Israel to the Jewish Diaspora should carry a Jewish message of hope in this darkest hour.[48]

The first group of nine dropped into Romania in March 1944. Chana Szenes's Hungarian group went on June 7, one day after the Allies landed on the beaches of Normandy and began the final assault against German troops in occupied Europe.

Chana Szenes did not survive her mission. She was captured and eventually executed, but she left a legacy to the people of Israel. In his introduction to the paperback edition of *Ordinary Heroes*, Peter Hay makes it clear that Chana had no illusions about the military success of her mission. She knew her chances ranged from small to nonexistent; she also knew that military success did not matter.

Chana felt that if just one Jew in hiding, in prison or in a concentration

---

## Unspeakable Things

*Even in Israel, Holocaust survivors felt set apart. In "Questions That Remain Unanswered," author and survivor Elie Wiesel explored the barrier that separates the Holocaust from ordinary experience. Wiesel's piece is taken from Tom Segev's* The Seventh Million.

"Even if you studied all the documentation, even if you listened to all the testimonies, visited all the camps and museums and read all the diaries, you would not be able to even approach the portal of that eternal night. This is the tragedy of the survivor's mission. He must tell a story that cannot be told. He must deliver a message that cannot be delivered. . . . In this sense the enemy, ironically, realized his goal. Since he extended the crime beyond all bounds, and since there is no way to cross those bounds except through language, it is impossible to tell the full story of his crime."

*Holocaust survivor and author Elie Wiesel.*

camp was given new courage by the fact that Jewish commandos dropped from the sky to bring aid, the mission would be worthwhile. That, and much more was accomplished. The example of the parachutists, the seven who died and the many more who survived, inspired generations of Israelis to take action into their own hands and to fight for what they love.[49]

## Ten Thousand Trucks

In the spring of 1944, another rescue proposal surfaced, this one far stranger than the mission that sent Chana Szenes and her comrades behind enemy lines. The idea started in the Hungarian capital of Bu-

*Chana Szenes, a volunteer paratrooper from Israel, penetrated Nazi territory in Hungary to aid Jews trapped there.*

dapest, soon after the Nazis had occupied the city. Joel Brand of the Hungarian Jewish Rescue Committee received a summons from Adolf Eichmann, the Nazi officer in charge of the "Final Solution" (Nazi term for the extermination of European Jews).

Eichmann wanted to make a deal: one million Hungarian Jews in exchange for "two hundred tons of tea, eight hundred tons of coffee, two million boxes of soap, ten thousand trucks, and a few unspecified . . . minerals."[50] He ordered Brand to carry the offer to the Allies. This was the beginning of the "trucks-for-blood" affair.

On May 19, Brand arrived in neutral Istanbul. He had been led to believe that Chaim Weizmann would be there to meet him. Instead, he landed in the middle of a bureaucratic tangle, unable to reach anyone with the authority to make a decision. When the Jewish Agency leadership finally heard of the proposal, they agreed that any chance to rescue a million Jews was worth a try.

The agency could not deliver such a large ransom on its own, so Ben-Gurion turned to the British for help. To his surprise, both the British and the Americans already knew about the proposal, through their own sources. They in turn notified their Russian allies.

Leaders of the three governments debated endlessly, trying to decide whether Eichmann's offer was genuine or a smokescreen for some hidden agenda of his own. While they talked, Eichmann was rounding up Jews at the rate of twelve thousand a day. Before long, there was nothing left to talk about and nobody left to save. The Jews of Hungary had been shipped to death camps.

Brand's ill-fated mission became a haunting footnote to the history of a troubled time. Was Eichmann's offer genuine,

## A Legacy of Death

*Heroic missions like that of paratrooper Chana Szenes could not hope to offset the terrible consequences of hatred, as Christopher Simpson explains in* The Splendid Blond Beast:

"The Nazis and their Hungarian collaborators carried out this destruction with greater speed, efficiency, and thoroughness than any comparable extermination in the Reich. Within ten days they deported some 116,000 Jews to Auschwitz, many of them families with children. They shipped 250,000 more people to extermination camps before the end of June. The Nazis gassed as many people as they could directly on arrival, but even Auschwitz's gas chambers could not keep up with the thousands of new victims who arrived each day."

or was it a cruel ruse? Could the Allies have done more? Could the Jewish Agency have stalled better? Nobody will ever know for sure. According to Brand's widow, those questions plagued her husband for the rest of his life (Brand died in 1964).

Hanzi Brand told Israeli journalist Tom Segev that her husband

> felt the need to tell over and over what had happened and how it had happened. That was how he dealt with the horrible feeling that hundreds of thousands of Jews had been murdered because his mission had failed. . . . He went around Tel Aviv for years with his story and not one journalist showed any interest. He believed all his life that the Jewish Agency leadership bore part of the guilt.[51]

On November 5, 1944, the war had turned against the Nazis, Allied troops marched toward Berlin, and Allied leaders were already making plans for after the war. According to British prime minister Winston

Churchill, those plans would include a Jewish state. He was prepared to support an agreement that would give the Jews "the whole of western Palestine."[52]

Weizmann was getting ready to take this news back to the Yishuv when he was summoned to an emergency meeting with colonial secretary Oliver Stanley. Lord Moyne, minister of state for the Middle East, had been gunned down in Cairo by Lehi extremists. The news stunned Weizmann and endangered everything he had achieved in his meetings with Winston Churchill.

The prime minister did not mince words when he spoke about the assassination before the House of Commons:

> If our dreams for Zionism are to end in the smoke of assassins' pistols, and our labours for its future to produce only a new set of gangsters worthy of Nazi Germany, many like myself will have to reconsider the position we have maintained so consistently and so long in the past.[53]

*The infamous "trucks-for-blood" mission of 1944 and its tragic outcome haunted Joel Brand for the rest of his life.*

In their stepped-up activity after the Biltmore conference in 1942, both the Irgun and Lehi organizations had stepped beyond the control of the Jewish Agency. Lehi seemed particularly addicted to violence, a legacy of its founder, Avraham Stern. The "Stern Gang," as Lehi was sometimes called, firmly believed that the ends justified the means. Sternists had been known to finance their illegal activities by extorting money from Jewish merchants and occasionally robbing a bank.

Chaim Weizmann was more than shocked that Jews would use such tactics; he was deeply wounded by what he saw as a betrayal of everything he believed. According to his autobiography *Trial and Error,* he saw

> a relaxation of the old, traditional Zionist purity of ethics, a touch of militarization, and a weakness for its trappings; here and there something worse—the tragic, futile un-Jewish resort to terror-

ism, a perversion of the purely defensive function of Haganah; and worst of all, in certain circles, a readiness to compound with the evil, to play politics with it, to condemn and not to condemn it, to treat it not as the thing it was, namely, an unmitigated curse to the National Home, but as a phenomenon which might have its advantages.[54]

## The Aftermath

On May 7, 1945 a beaten Germany offered her unconditional surrender to the Allies. The war in Europe was over, and everyone rejoiced. Then came the counting of the Jewish dead, and a stunned world learned the true cost of Hitler's "Final Solution"— 6 million human lives.

According to the *American Jewish Yearbook, 1947-48,* the Jewish population of Europe in 1939 was 9,739,200; in 1947 it was down to 3,920,100. Even after these facts became known, the Allies were slow to create a Jewish nation in Palestine. Weizmann appealed to Churchill, but the British prime minister was not ready to carry the Zionist cause before the court of world opinion. Perhaps he sensed that the time was not right, perhaps he was still bitter about the Moyne assassination.

Regardless of Churchill's motives, the outcome was the same: once more the Jewish national home had been pushed aside for other priorities. Chaim Weizmann took this as a personal failure: "I stand before young Jews today," he once said, "as a leader who failed to achieve anything by peaceful means."[55] In Palestine, the younger generation of Zionists was preparing to move beyond those peaceful means.

# 6 Fighting for the Dream

Postwar Europe was in shambles, faced with restoring cities, economies, and lives. Gentile survivors returned to what was left of their homes and began the long, slow process of rebuilding. Most Jewish survivors had no place to go. Their homes were destroyed, their families dead, the life they had known was gone forever. Thousands ended up in Displaced Persons (D.P.) camps, waiting for news that someone, somewhere, was prepared to take them in.

## Saving the 100,000

These traumatized survivors needed more than a place to go: they needed help to rejoin the world of the living. According to Francesca Wilson, who worked in a D.P. facility,

> at first it was hard to look at [the survivors] without repulsion. I have seen

*Jews who survived the horrors of World War II ended up in D.P. camps, such as this one in Germany.*

victims of famine before: Bulgarian prisoners in Serbia, Russians in the Volga area in 1922, children in Vienna in 1919 and in Spain in the Civil War—but this was worse, for these people were victims of cruelty. . . . They had the furtive look and gestures of hunted animals. By years of brutal treatment, by the murder of relatives, by the constant fear of death, all that was human had been taken away from them . . . nothing would persuade them to eat in communal dining rooms. I noticed an old man who was trying to eat but was too weak to finish his food. Three boys were staring at his plate. I had once seen the same look of burning yet cautious intentness on the face of a wolf that was following my sleigh on the Russian steppes.[56]

The surviving European Jews had to be helped, and David Ben-Gurion meant to do so. After the British elections of July 1945 put Clement Attlee and his Labor Party into power, Ben-Gurion led a delegation to London, where he met with new colonial secretary, George Hall.

Lacking Chaim Weizmann's homey charm and diplomatic skills, Ben-Gurion was frank to the point of rudeness. He presented Hall with a list of demands, including most of the points of the Biltmore Program along with a request that 100,000 Jewish displaced persons be immediately admitted to Palestine.

Hall was outraged by the scope of the demands and by Ben-Gurion's blunt aggressiveness, which he described as "different from anything which I had ever before experienced."[57] Thus the negotiations fell apart before they even started. Politicians continued to dicker about what to do, while victims of Nazi terror languished in D.P. camps.

## Investigating the Horror

Accounts of survivors warehoused by the thousands in D.P. camps disturbed U.S. president Harry Truman. Shortly after Ben-Gurion's disastrous mission, Truman sent Earl G. Harrison, dean of the University of Pennsylvania Law School and a former commissioner of immigration, to investigate the D.P. camps, talk with Holocaust survivors, and report on what he found.

The result of Harrison's investigation was

an exceedingly moving document describing misery that, as Truman said, "could not be allowed to continue." And [the report] reinforced [Truman's] belief that Palestine was the answer. Palestine, reported Harrison, was "definitely and preeminently" the choice of the Jewish survivors in Europe. Only in Palestine would "they be welcomed and find peace and quiet and be given an opportunity to live and work. No other single matter is, therefore, so important from the viewpoint of Jews in Germany and Austria and those elsewhere who have known the horrors of concentration camps as is the disposition of the Palestine question."[58]

The Jewish underground refused to wait while the Allies grappled with political and philosophical niceties. By the autumn of 1945, Haganah, Irgun, and the Stern Gang were all active in an increasingly militant resistance movement. Commandos attacked a British detention camp to free several hundred illegal immigrants. They bombed railroad tracks to stop British troop movements, sabotaged airfields and

## Miriam's Story

*For Holocaust survivors like Miriam Weinfeld, the new life in Israel was all too often haunted by an old life they would rather forget. Tom Segev tells of one survivor's poignant rescue in* The Seventh Million:

"Toward the end of the war, Miriam Weinfeld turned seventeen. In the days before the German surrender, she was taken on the death march from Auschwitz to Bergen-Belsen. Her mental anguish, particularly her inability to help her mother, had been harder to bear than the physical hardship, she later recalled. Conditions in Bergen-Belsen in the weeks before the camp was liberated were even worse than they had been in the past. Her mother died before her eyes. When the British soldiers finally arrived, wearing gas masks against the stench of the tens of thousands of corpses strewn around the barracks, Weinfeld's first thought was, 'Too bad they came so late.' There was nothing left to save."

communication facilities, destroyed naval patrol boats that intercepted refugee vessels. Britain responded in force, sending troops to fortify their garrisons and naval vessels to blockade the coastline.

## Reasoning Together: The Anglo-American Committee

By the spring of 1946, a troublesome situation had become an explosive one. Caught between Arabs who threatened violence if the British allowed mass immigration and Jews who threatened violence if they did not allow it, Prime Minister Attlee contacted President Truman. The two leaders agreed to form a joint committee to investigate the problem of Jewish refugees, and devise a plan that would not plunge a good portion of the world into another war.

Thus began the Anglo-American Committee of Inquiry. To get the widest possible view of the situation, the committee held hearings in the United States, Europe, and Palestine. Both Jews and Arabs made convincing cases for their positions. Azzam Pasha, secretary general of the Arab League, had once advocated a dialogue of reconciliation with the Jews. By the time he spoke to the committee, his position had hardened:

> The Zionist, the new Jew . . . pretends that he has got a particular civilizing mission with which he returns to a backward, degenerate race [Arabs] in order to put the elements of progress into an area which has no progress. Well . . . the Arabs simply stand and say "No." . . . We are a living, vitally strong

nation, we are in our renaissance. . . . We have a heritage of civilization and of spiritual life. We are not going to allow ourselves to be controlled either by great nations or small nations or dispersed nations.[59]

Chaim Weizmann based his testimony on Jewish history in the diaspora and on the anti-Semitism that never seemed to go away. It would not go away, he said, so long as Jews lived among the peoples of the world as a nation without a home. In the aftermath of the Nazi horror, Weizmann felt a sovereign state was necessary to the survival of the Jewish people.

He made an impassioned yet well-reasoned case for the Yishuv, pointing out its accomplishments, its creativity, its service to the Allied cause during the war. Weizmann concluded his testimony with an assertion so honest and reasonable it stunned the entire committee. According to British delegate Richard Crossman, Weizmann was "the first witness who frankly and openly admitted that the issue is not between right and wrong but between the greater and lesser injustice."[60]

Other witnesses provided hard data about the Yishuv's economic and technological growth, produced charts and graphs to show that Palestine could absorb more than a million immigrants within ten years, and even supplied hydrological studies to show that water supplies would be adequate for this larger population.

## The Committee's Report

The committee report was completed by May 1. It acknowledged the plight of Holo-

*A photo dated April 11, 1946, shows an informal talk at the Anglo-American Inquiry.*

caust survivors and recommended that the mandate authority immediately issue the much-disputed 100,000 immigration certificates. Proposals for the longer term envisioned United Nations trusteeship over a Palestine that would be neither Arab nor Jewish but unified to include both. Until unification could be achieved, the British mandatory government would continue to administer the country.

In trying to harmonize competing interests, the Anglo-American Committee managed to offend everyone. The Arabs did not want 100,000 Jewish immigrants, and the Jews did not want to be governed by a U.N. trusteeship. The British simply wanted out; maintaining the mandate was a drain on financial reserves that the war had already exhausted.

For President Truman, political and economic considerations paled beside the humanitarian issues of the refugee problem. On the day the Anglo-American Report was published in Washington, he gave it his wholehearted endorsement and called for the immediate admission of 100,000 Jewish refugees into Palestine.

The Attlee government in Britain was furious that Truman had made a public statement without consulting them first. Attlee's foreign secretary Ernest Bevin, a man more accustomed to rough-and-tumble labor organizing than the niceties of international diplomacy, dismissed Truman's action as "a crude desire for votes in [the Jewish community] of New York and suggested Truman had no wish to see more Jews coming to the Unites States."[61]

Bevin went on to offend the ever-reasonable Chaim Weizmann with a reference to "pushy Jews" wanting to "get too much at the head of the [line]."[62] There would be no mass immigration so long as Britain governed Palestine, Bevin maintained. This became the official position of the British Government.

## Beyond Compromise: The Specter of Violence

On May 12, 1946, the Jewish underground issued a challenge of its own. In an underground radio broadcast, Hanganah warned the British government that if it did not fulfill

its responsibilities under the mandate—above all with regard to the question of immigration—the Jewish Resistance Movement will make every effort to hinder the transfer of British bases to Palestine and to prevent their establishment in this country.[63]

The resistance stepped up its attacks against British installations. On June 17, in a series of coordinated assaults known as "The Night of the Bridges," Haganah strike teams blew up ten of the eleven bridges that connected Palestine with neighboring nations.

On Saturday, June 29, a day the Yishuv would remember as the "Black Sabbath," British troops responded in force, ransacking any structure that might have been a resistance hideout, including homes, schools, and hospitals. Along the way they

*British foreign secretary Ernest Bevin opposed mass immigration of Jews to Palestine, as did the British mandate government in the country.*

arrested and detained twenty-seven hundred people suspected of underground activity. The constant searches paralyzed the entire resistance movement.

The Jewish reaction to these events all but destroyed the uncomfortable alliance of the Jewish defense groups, Haganah, Irgun, and Lehi. Haganah planned no retaliation for the Black Sabbath operation. Jewish Agency president David Ben-Gurion sensed that to do so would only provoke harsher measures; better to let tempers cool so the British would relax their vigilance and give the Yishuv some breathing space.

Irgun did not agree. The organization's commander, Menachem Begin, was

an intense, angry young man who once served time in a Siberian labor camp. He had no interest in "cooling off" periods. He planned an operation that would grab headlines all over the world: the bombing of British military headquarters, which occupied an entire wing of the King David Hotel in Jerusalem. According to a 1996 article in the *Jerusalem Post*,

> three warnings were issued prior to the execution of the operation. . . . The first was a call to the King David itself, where the message was received by the telephone operator, the second to the offices of the *Palestine Post* [a newspaper], and the third to the nearby French consulate. All three places later confirmed they received these warnings calling for a complete evacuation of the hotel. But the building was not evacuated.[64]

British authorities denied receiving any warning. At precisely 12:37 P.M. the bombs exploded, "demolishing the entire southwest wing of the building."[65] The charred shell of the building became a symbol of the strife that was tearing Palestine apart. Ninety-one people died in the blast. Both Chaim Weizmann and David Ben-Gurion denounced the bombing as an act of terrorism.

After the bombing, the outraged British placed all of Palestine under what amounted to martial law, or emergency military rule. They imposed a curfew in Tel Aviv and Jerusalem and ordered patrols to shoot violators on the spot. Commanding General Sir Evelyn Barker declared Jewish shops and homes off limits to British personnel.

In the swirl of controversy about terrorist tactics, Haganah became increasingly involved in what Howard Sachar

*The King David Hotel in Jerusalem is shown here in the aftermath of the Irgun's bombing. Despite three reported warnings, the building was not evacuated, and ninety-one people died.*

called "a far more compelling and effective method for undermining British policy in the Holy Land"[66]—in other words, illegal immigration. Between the end of the war in 1945 and the Israeli declaration of independence in 1948, approximately 140 immigrant ships, carrying some 70,000 Holocaust survivors, tried to run the British naval blockade.

## The *Exodus*

The best known of these voyages was that of the *Exodus,* a battered cruise ship that had seen duty as a troop transport during World War II. Haganah bought it for $50,000 and transformed it into an enduring symbol of freedom, as described by Tom Segev:

Its purchase, outfitting, the swearing in of its crew, even the details of its mission, were no secret. American newspapermen were invited to cover the story, which included ceremonies and celebrations preceding the sailing. From the very start, it was intended as a public-relations tool for the Zionist movement.[67]

The ship served that purpose well. The odyssey of *Exodus* had all the ingredients of high drama: an idealistic, volunteer crew, forty-five hundred survivors of unthinkable atrocities, and a powerful empire determined to keep them out of their ancestral homeland.

*Exodus* embarked from Port-de-Bouc, France, on July 9, 1947. On July 18, while still in international waters off the coast of Haifa, she was surrounded by six British

## Running Risks

*The illegal immigration of Holocaust survivors was a dangerous operation, as this May 1946 article from* Time *magazine makes clear:*

"Only Jehovah knew last week how many Jews were moving out of their modern bondage toward the ancient promised land. By thousands they fled from eastern Europe, where three-fourths of the Continent's 1,300,000 surviving Jews (not including those of Russia) have found no victory in Hitler's defeat. Their exodus was illegal, clandestine, and humanitarian. A Polish Jewess explained why: 'You know what Europe is to me? It's a cemetery. When I walk into a store and see soap on sale, I remember that this may be the body of my sister.'

Landing in Palestine is a touch-&-go operation. The vigilant British patrol is composed of coast guard stations on 24-hour watch, motor launches and cutters, radar posts. If a ship eludes all these, the authorities may throw a smoke screen around a suspected landing place, then intensively search nearby homes and fields. . . . Haganah men say that in the last four months they brought 7,000 out of 10,000 'illegals' safely through the British Cordon."

battleships. One of them rammed her hull and in the resulting confusion, armed British sailors swarmed aboard. When the passengers fought back, the boarding party opened fire. Three refugees died that day; dozens were injured.

Although world opinion turned against the British, they refused to yield. They loaded the refugees into three smaller ships and took them back to Port-de-Bouc. The passengers flatly refused to disembark, and the French would not allow them to be taken off against their will. Tom Segev wrote:

The drama lasted three weeks. Journalists from around the world . . . described the would-be immigrants as prisoners in a "floating Auschwitz" [largest and most infamous of the Nazi death camps]. The world had not been swept by such a wave of sympathy for Jewish suffering since the day the first reporters entered the concentration camps.[68]

Faced with an impasse that was becoming awkward and even dangerous, the British made a move that aroused indignation all over the world: they sent forty-five thousand Holocaust survivors to Germany. So it was that the people aboard the *Exodus* found themselves interned "on the shores of a 'cursed' country, as they called Germany, in two fenced-in camps not far from Lübeck on the Baltic seacoast."[69]

## The Rocky Road to Nationhood

Those turbulent days marked the lives of everyone who lived through them. In 1997, surviving crewmen and passengers of the *Exodus* gathered to commemorate the fiftieth anniversary of their famous voyage and to reflect upon its meaning. "By many accounts, the post-war clandestine immigration movement . . . was instrumental in forcing the British to relinquish control of Palestine in May 1948,"[70] wrote journalist Michele Chabin in a *USA Today* article about the reunion. As retired Israeli army officer Uzi Narkiss recalled:

> Members of the U.N. committee sent to Palestine to research the prospects of partitioning the country watched the *Exodus* struggle unfold from their balconies in Haifa. . . . I'm certain much of their decision to establish a Jewish state came out of that experience.[71]

Many observers would agree with Narkiss. The *Exodus* saga was still in the minds of U.N. delegates on November 29,

*British soldiers board the Jewish immigrant ship* Exodus *near Haifa. The battered ship was not allowed to dock, and the passengers were eventually taken to refugee camps in Germany.*

1947, when they voted to partition Palestine into independent Jewish and Arab states. Britain immediately announced that it would terminate the mandate in stages, making a final withdrawal of all troops on May 15, 1948. Not even David Ben-Gurion had expected the British to withdraw so quickly. In a flurry of activity, the Jews began laying the groundwork for a future without the mandate authority.

The Arab reaction was equally swift and was targeted toward disrupting the partition of Palestine by any means possible. From all over the Arab world came angry denunciations of the United Nations, the Jews, and the partition resolution. Al-Haji Amin al-Husayni of a militant Palestinian nationalist group known as the Arab Higher Committee declared United Nations Resolution 181 "null and void,"[72] and vowed to fight it in every way.

In Palestine, an Arab Liberation Army suddenly appeared as a staunch adversary of the Jews. Arab troops laid siege to the Jewish neighborhoods of Jerusalem, drawing a cordon so tight that the Haganah

---

## The Story of Deir Yassin

*On April 9, 1948, a combined force of Irgun and Lehi commandos attacked the Arab village of Deir Yassin. According to Menachem Begin, who commanded the operation, what followed was a battle. According to other sources, it was a massacre. Meir Pa'il, a Haganah officer who observed the assault, made the following statement, which is quoted in David Shipler's Arab and Jew.*

"It was a massacre in hot blood, it was not pre-planned. It was an outburst from below with no one to control it. Groups of men went from house to house looting and shooting, shooting and looting. You could hear the cries from within the houses of Arab women, Arab elders, Arab kids. I tried to find the commanders, but I did not succeed. I tried to shout and to hold them, but they took no notice. Their eyes were glazed. It was as if they were drugged, mentally poisoned, in ecstasy.

Pa'il took . . . pictures and wrote a report to his superiors, beginning with the first lines of a Hebrew poem composed by Chaim Nachman Bialik following the 1903 pogrom in Kishinev, in which forty-nine Jews were killed and five hundred injured by a Russian mob:

'Arise and go to the city of the killing and you
   will come to the courtyards,
and with your eyes you will see and with your
   hands you will feel on the fences
and on the trees and on the stones and on the
   plaster
the congealed blood . . . of the slain.'"

could not break it. In the city, Jews suffered through a terrible winter, struggling to survive on existing supplies of food and fuel.

Haganah kept fighting until they broke the siege of Jerusalem and gained control of much of the surrounding territory. Irgun and Lehi staged raids of their own to insure Jewish control of strategically important sites. Some of those raids seemed more like terrorist attacks.

## Massacre at Deir Yassin

Whenever Israelis talk about the atrocities of their various wars, the name of Deir Yassin is always mentioned. Deir Yassin was an Arab village about five miles west of Jerusalem. On April 9, 1948, a combined Irgun-Lehi assault group attacked the village and killed 254 unarmed civilians, including about 100 women and children.

"The massacre at Deir Yassin," wrote Israeli journalist Tom Segev, "became a landmark in the chronicles of the Israeli-Arab conflict and a symbol of the horrors of war."[73] Both the Jewish Agency and Haganah issued statements condemning the attack on Deir Yassin. David Ben-Gurion sent King Abdullah of Jordan a message of apology and regret.

Some people claimed that Deir Yassin was a legitimate military target; the massacre, a battle that went wrong, as described by Israeli scholar Benny Morris:

[T]he weight of the evidence suggests that the dissident troops did not go in [to Deir Yassin] with the intention of committing a massacre but lost their

*This photo, taken the day after the Irgun-Lehi massacre of Arab civilians at Deir Yassin, shows survivors of the attack wandering in search of a new home.*

heads during the battle, which they found unexpectedly tough-going.[74]

Others suspect that the attack was neither a legitimate military operation nor an unintentional massacre, but a calculated attempt to drive Palestinian Arabs out of the future Jewish state. Menachem Begin openly stated that Deir Yassin aided the cause of Jewish conquest. In his book about the Irgun, he recalls the Jewish entry into Haifa, when "the Arabs began to flee in panic, shouting 'Deir Yassin.'"[75]

Whether or not Deir Yassin was part of a plot to drive the Arabs from their homes, it helped to create a climate of terror. As the Jews advanced, Arabs fled their homes. Tens of thousands packed what few possessions they could carry and sought sanctuary in neighboring nations and in Arab-controlled areas of Palestine. This was the beginning of a refugee problem that would plague the Middle East for decades.

# Chapter

# 7 Building a Nation

With the end of British administration approaching in May 1948, the leaders of the Yishuv faced an important question: should they declare independence as soon as the British leave? Some cautioned against such a move, arguing that it would invite an Arab attack in force. The Yishuv was not strong enough to fight a war for its very existence.

## First Steps to Freedom

David Ben-Gurion listened to arguments on both sides. His own inclinations were to declare independence immediately, while the timing seemed right. For once in his public career, the advice he most wanted was from the man who had been his adversary for many years: Chaim Weizmann. At the time, Weizmann was in the United States, reinforcing American support for the partition resolution.

According to legend, Ben-Gurion summoned Weizmann's assistant, Meyer Weisgal, to an emergency meeting. "I must know *at once* what Weizmann thinks about declaring independence," he said. Weisgal went all the way to Nice, France, to make the transatlantic call on an untapped phone. "Weizmann's reply was blunt and in style: 'What are they waiting for, the idiots?'"[76]

On May 14, 1948, with the British mandate scheduled to end at midnight, four hundred people gathered in the Tel Aviv Museum for the formal reading of their Declaration of Independence. On a platform sat representatives of the new state's provisional government (appointed to serve until elections could be held). Behind them hung the Zionist flag: white, with a pale blue six-pointed Jewish star centered between two pale blue lines. That day it became the flag of the independent State of Israel.

The ceremonies began with the haunting strains of "Hatikvah" (in English, "The Hope"), an anthem that had been sung at Zionist gatherings since the days of Theodore Herzl. At 4:00 P.M., David Ben-Gurion began to read the Declaration of Independence. "As he reached the words proclaiming 'the establishment of the Jewish State in Palestine, to be called Israel,' the audience cheered and wept."[77]

By morning, the new nation was under attack by the armies of Egypt, Jordan, Iraq, and Syria, fighting for its life in a battle many believed it could never hope to win.

Israel's first year of existence was a harrowing test of its national character. The new nation struggled to build a society and protect it from enemies that refused to acknowledge its right to exist. Israel's war of independence lasted for eight months

# An Anthem of Hope

*In his book* A Treasury of Jewish Inspirational Stories, *Lawrence Epstein tells the story of Israel's national anthem and the man who wrote it.*

"Every Israeli schoolchild knows the words to the Israeli national anthem, '*Hatikvah.*' The somber, stirring melody and the stirring words . . . are more well known than the author of the anthem.

Naphtali Herz Imber (1856–1909) was born in Zloczov, Galicia, to a devout [religious] family. He began his poetic endeavors early, winning recognition in 1870 for a poem centered on Austrian patriotism. After his father died, Imber began almost a life of wandering, going to Vienna and then to Constantinople. Imber probably wrote '*Hatikvah*' in 1878 in Jassy, Romania, probably after hearing of the founding of [the Jewish village] Petah Tikvah, which inspired his imagination. . . .

Imber never lived to see his beloved poem officially adopted as the anthem of the Zionist movement, but he did know of its influence. There had been calls for an open competition for such an anthem in Herzl's Zionist paper *Die Welt* as early as 1898. The Second Zionist Congress in 1898 and the Congress in 1900 debated about an anthem, but they could not reach an agreement. '*Hatikvah*' was sung at the conclusion of one of the sessions of the Fifth Zionist Congress in 1901, and a group of dissidents sang it at the Sixth Congress in 1903. It was only at the Seventh Zionist Congress in 1905 that all those present sang '*Hatikvah*' and were enormously moved by its power. The overwhelming reception made it the movement's unofficial song, but it was not officially adopted until 1933.

On May 14, 1948, '*Hatikvah*' was sung at the opening of the ceremony to declare the new state of Israel, and the symphony orchestra played it at the conclusion of the ceremony. Since then it has been recognized by Jews around the world as the anthem that best expresses the yearning of the Jewish people for a national homeland and a confirmation of the centrality of Israel in Jewish life."

*David Ben-Gurion reads the Declaration of Independence on May 14, 1948; the day Britain ended its mandate government and the Jewish nation of Israel was established.*

overall and surprised the military experts who had predicted swift defeat.

By all accepted standards, the Arab armies should have quickly dispatched Israel. They had air support, superior weaponry, and career officers in command of their troops. Israeli defense forces had citizen-soldiers, obsolete weaponry, and no air force to relieve the pressure on ground troops. On the day of the invasion, Haganah was desperately trying to assemble weaponry and ammunition.

The Arabs had every confidence that they could conquer the Israelis with little difficulty. According to one commander, they were in high spirits as they marched off to battle:

It was a sultry May day, with a haze of dust hanging over the roads. In the city of Amman [Jordan] and in every village along the road the people were gathered, cheering and clapping wildly

as each unit drove past. The flat roofs and the windows were crowded with women and children, whose shrill cries and wavering trebles could be heard above the roar and the rattle of the vehicles, and the cheering of the crowds of men beside the road. The troops themselves were in jubilation. In some trucks, the soldiers were clapping and cheering. In others, they were laughing and waving to the crowds as they passed. Many of the vehicles had been decorated with green branches or bunches of pink oleander flowers, which grew beside the road. The procession seemed more like a carnival than an army going to war.[78]

The Israelis did not have a formal chain of command, or the pageantry of an army marching off to war. They did not even have uniforms. They fought as commando units, using the arts of concealment and surprise to strike the enemy when they least expected it. In some parts of the country, troops found help from kibbutzniks (members of collective farming communities). These people of all ages and both sexes fought fiercely to protect their settlements. Sometimes these civilian fighters made the difference between defeat and victory. For example, the people of Kibbutz Yad Mordechai grappled with almost half of the Egyptian coastal forces for six days. During this time, Haganah commander Yigael Yadin was able to plan the defense of Tel Aviv.

Tel Aviv was the largest Jewish city in Palestine, a center of commerce, industry, and government. If it fell to Egyptian forces, the Israeli cause would be doomed. Yadin knew this; he also knew that the Egyptians would soon be in striking range of the city. He could not hope to defeat them on the field of battle, so he devised a plan that relied upon surprise, misdirection, and the natural tendency of many people to believe the international newswires.

## Unorthodox Tactics

In darkness, Yadin staged a huge, noisy, and dramatic raid on the Egyptian flank. While the camp was in disarray, he released press announcements to every news service in the

### Healing Laughter

*Even the most desperate situations generate their own special humor. This anecdote from Bernard Raskas's* Heart of Wisdom Book III *touches a lighter side of the Israeli struggle for nationhood.*

"During the 1948 War of Independence, there were chronic shortages. Israeli soldiers had to make do with what they had, often having to train with pretend weapons.

Once, during the war, a young man was on guard duty. Unfortunately, there was no ammunition available, so the guard was provided with a broom and told to pretend that it was a machine gun in case the Arabs attacked.

Only a short time later, the guard first heard footsteps and then saw soldiers advancing toward him. He shouted out for the soldiers to stop or be killed. The soldiers, however, continued to advance.

It was only when they got close that the guard realized they were Israelis. Indeed, the guard's brother was leading the soldiers. The guard turned to his brother and said, 'Why didn't you stop. You could have been killed.'

The brother said, 'You couldn't have hurt me. You see, I am a tank.'"

Middle East: in a massive thrust by superior combat units, the Israeli army had cut Egyptian supply lines along the coast, ending the threat to Tel Aviv. The ruse worked as Yadin had hoped. Egyptian High Command flashed orders to the field commanders to halt and hold position.

Inland from Tel Aviv, a daring young officer named Moshe Dayan held off an entire armored column with a pair of salvaged howitzer cannons from the Franco-Prussian War of 1870. Dayan was already a seasoned fighter with the scars to prove it. As a member of the British forces in World War II, he lost an eye during a vital reconnaissance mission into enemy territory. The resulting black patch gave him a swashbuckling image that seemed to match his unorthodox battle tactics.

His tactic at Degania was bold yet simple: convince the enemy that he had a well-fortified position with firepower to spare. A barrage from two elderly howitzers would not fool anybody, so Dayan held his fire as the column advanced. When it was well within range, he lobbed a single shell directly into the lead tank. The tank exploded, making an awesome display. Behind it, the column came to an abrupt halt, then retreated. Degania was safe.

## Stand at Yad Mordechai

*When a kibbutz was all that stood between the advancing Egyptian army and the city of Tel Aviv, a small group of fighters held their ground for six days, as Amos Elon explains in* The Israelis: Founders and Sons:

"There were barely over a hundred men at Yad Mordechai, including boys of fourteen years; only about seventy-five or eighty men and boys were capable fighters. Armed only with rifles, some of them antiquated, 3,000 rounds of ammunition, 400 hand grenades, two machine guns, two-inch mortars with 50 shells, the defenders of Yad Mordechai effectively blocked the advance of a whole Egyptian brigade for a full six days. . . . Teen-agers with homemade Molotov bottles threw themselves upon Egyptian tanks and armored vehicles. The settlement was surrounded and under constant artillery fire and it was repeatedly bombed from the air. Twenty-four men—nearly one-third of the active defending force—were killed; another thirty were wounded. . . . On [the fifth day], the last machine gun had become unserviceable. Late that night, the men of Yad Mordechai decided to abandon their burning settlement. . . . The survivors managed . . . [to reach] the neighboring settlement of Gvar Am, a few miles north."

*Israeli military officer Moshe Dayan successfully defended the Degania kibbutz from the Syrian army.*

## Temporary Cease-Fire

Through such maneuvers early in the war, the Israelis managed to hide their lack of firepower and stave off disaster. In the process, they forced the Arabs to stretch their resources to the limit. Both sides were ready to listen when U.N. mediator Count Folke Bernadotte came to Palestine to negotiate a temporary cease-fire.

Bernadotte, a Swede with long experience in delicate negotiations, promptly hit an impasse with the Israelis. They would not agree to any limitations on immigration during the cease-fire period. Undaunted, Bernadotte worked out a compromise: neither side could bring in troops or weapons, and male immigrants of military age would live in camps under U.N. supervision. With this change, the combatants agreed to cease hostilities on June 11, 1948.

## Truce, Tragedy, and Confrontation

Both sides were less than dutiful in observing the restrictions. The Arabs sent thirteen thousand new recruits and tons of war matériel into the combat zone, while Haganah brought in everything from ammunition to field artillery and fighter planes. Most of the equipment was purchased from sympathetic Czech and French sources.

Irgun also made arms deals, acting independently of both Haganah and the provisional government. Under Menachem Begin, Irgun had continued to take a right-wing position, supporting militant Jewish nationalism without concessions to the Arabs or to the United Nations. In June 1948, this aggressive posture triggered a confrontation that nearly plunged Israel into a disastrous civil war.

The trouble began with a surplus ship called *Altalena,* which left France with some nine hundred military recruits and a cargo of rifles, machine guns, and "millions of rounds of ammunition."[79] Though landing that cargo in Palestine would violate the truce, Irgun refused to order the ship to turn back or put in at a neutral port.

Sources differ about the sequence of events as the *Altalena* approached the Israeli coastline. Frantic radio messages warned *Altalena* not to attempt to land her forbidden cargo. Some say these messages were genuine; others considered them a blind, sent in the interests of appearances. Historian Howard Sachar states that David Ben-Gurion authorized a secret landing, but withdrew his permission when Irgun "demanded that 20 percent of the weapons go to its own units."[80]

*Irgun awaits inspection by Menachem Begin during a parade in Jerusalem. Irgun, led by Begin, attempted to land the* Altalena's *forbidden arms and troops in Israel.*

In her 1994 documentary *Altalena,* Israeli filmmaker Ilana Tsur treats the message as genuine. She interviews the radio operator who actually sent that famous message,

> telling [the *Altalena*] urgently to keep away from Israel, in accordance with the first cease fire of the War of Independence. [The operator] recalls how she tried to send the message in code and, receiving no reply, sent an open and uncoded message, telling the ship to keep away and await instructions. The *Altalena* either did not receive or did not obey the command.[81]

One way or another, Irgun defied the authority of the Israeli government, and that, David Ben-Gurion simply refused to allow. When *Altalena* tried to land in Tel Aviv, all the elements of the confrontation were in place: Ben-Gurion defending the authority of the infant state, Menachem Begin attempting to land his contraband cargo, and Yitzhak Rabin commanding the troops that stood between them. Each of these men had the interests of Israel at heart; each of them would one day serve as prime minister.

## The Fate of the *Altalena*

On that day, each leader played a role in an epic confrontation. Ben-Gurion's orders were clear: take any measures necessary to prevent the ship from landing. Menachem Begin refused to back down. As *Altalena* headed into port, Rabin's artillery opened fire. *Altalena*'s guns answered. The result was a fiece firefight that ended with *Altalena* exploding into flames. According to Howard Sachar, twelve of the ship's crew and seventy recruits perished in the flames.

Uri Yarom, who was attached to Rabin's troops at the time, recalled images of horror: "I'll never forget that there were people on our side who waited for a chance to spot heads above the water—and shoot them. . . . They shot wounded people, it's true."[82]

The situation was beyond anyone's control and heading for disaster when a shaky but still defiant Menachem Begin went on radio to give an impassioned order to his followers: under no circumstances should they engage in civil war. Israelis remember that epic announcement as the "speech of tears," in which the fiery young revolutionary placed the survival of the newborn nation above his own political agenda.

In the aftermath of the *Altalena* affair, David Ben-Gurion outlawed Irgun and transformed Haganah's loose alliance of commando squads into the Israel Defense Forces (IDF), an efficient and disciplined military force with sixty thousand troops and a respectable arsenal of weaponry.

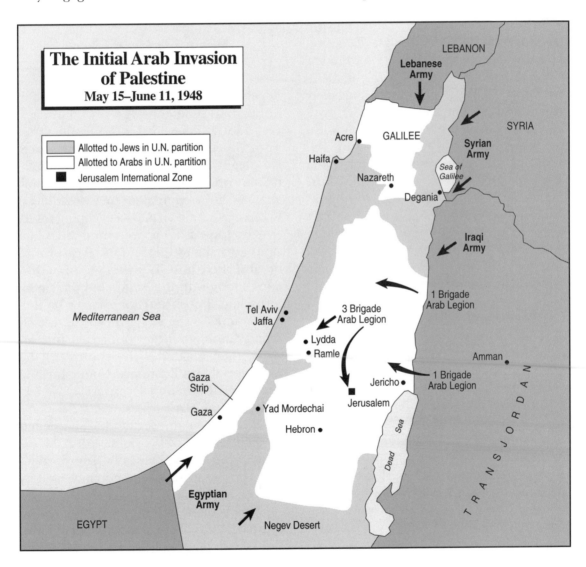

**The Initial Arab Invasion of Palestine**
May 15–June 11, 1948

Allotted to Jews in U.N. partition
Allotted to Arabs in U.N. partition
■ Jerusalem International Zone

## The Ten Days War

On July 8, 1948, Egyptian forces under General Muhammad Naguib moved on Israeli positions in the south, bringing an early end to the cease-fire. The Israeli defense system responded in force, pounding the main Egyptian line until General Naguib had no choice but to fall back. The conflict was a minor victory for Israel but a sign of things to come.

In just ten days of fierce fighting, the IDF took Arab territory all over Palestine, capturing the town of Nazareth and much of the lower Galilee. These captures secured the IDF position in the strategically critical Lydda-Ramle area. On July 11, Lydda's international airport fell to troops under the command of Moshe Dayan, the same man who once saved Kibbutz Degania with a pair of seventy-year-old howitzers. These changes in Israeli fortunes triggered a new militant attitude toward Palestinian Arabs. In each newly conquered territory, the Israelis encouraged local Arabs to leave. One popular form of pressure was a steady stream of threats, warnings, and rumors, all calculated to spread terror through the Arab population.

This psychological warfare cleared many villages without a shot being fired; it also began to change the population patterns of the country. By the time the War of Independence ended, 750,000 Palestinian Arabs would have been forced out of their homes. Six months later, that figure would rise to 940,000.

As Palestinian refugees flooded into surrounding countries and more territory fell to the Jews, diplomatic observers became alarmed. This "small" war was getting out of hand. U.N. mediator Folke Bernadotte sensed that the time had come for quick and decisive action. On July 15, the U.N. Security Council met in emergency session. By unanimous vote, it ordered a cease-fire to begin on July 18.

This truce was not negotiated as the first one had been. It was imposed by the United Nations and enforced with threats of severe economic sanctions. Thus ended the portion of the Arab-Israeli conflict that would become known as the Ten Days War.

## Bernadotte's Plan

Bernadotte ensured that the latest cease-fire had no time limit. A career diplomat, Bernadotte believed that he could transform this truce into a permanent peace. He organized a large staff of international military observers and technical personnel, along with the equipment they would need to serve as a long-term peacekeeping force.

On June 27, he presented his plan, calling for Palestinian Arab territories to be absorbed into Transjordan (now Jordan), along with the Negev and the city of Jerusalem. Jewish territory was to be limited mainly to the western Galilee. Jewish immigration would be unlimited for two years, then go under the control of the U.N. Social and Economic Council. Haifa and the international airport at Lydda would become free zones.

With this plan, Bernadotte succeeded in alienating all of the political leaders except King Abdullah of Transjordan. Bernadotte was shocked and chastened by the general outcry.

Not to be defeated by this blunder, he created a new proposal, which would give the Israelis national sovereignty over the

*U.N. mediator Count Folke Bernadotte (right) with Israeli foreign minister Moshe Shertok in June 1948. Bernadotte was asassinated a few months later.*

entire Galilee, give the Negev to the Arabs, and make Jerusalem an international city that would be under direct authority of the United Nations. He presented this new report on September 16, only to have it meet the fate of the earlier proposal.

The next day, Bernadotte's staff car was waylaid by four men in the uniforms of Jewish soldiers. One of them fired into the car at point-blank, killing Bernadotte and another U.N. official. Lehi was implicated in the assassinations, but the actual attackers were never found.

The Israeli government conducted a nationwide roundup of Lehi members, arresting more than four hundred, including Nathan Friedmann-Yellin, the man who had led Lehi since the death of its notorious founder, Avraham Stern. Despite this fast action, Israel lost sympathy in the United Nations.

In the wake of Bernadotte's death, any hope for an immediate truce was doomed. For weeks the Israelis stockpiled equipment and mobilized troops for a new offensive in the Negev. They struck on October 14, claiming that Egyptian troops had destroyed an unarmed convoy that was taking supplies to southern kibbutzim. Later sources state that the Israelis dynamited the trucks themselves, to destroy the tottering cease-fire and launch what would prove to be their last offensive of the war.

Under command of Yigal Allon, gifted battlefield strategist, Israeli troops moved swiftly through the Negev, forcing the Egyptians back to their fortified positions just north of the Sinai frontier. There, the Egyptians braced for a frontal assault that never came. Allon sent an armored column against one side of the line and an infantry brigade with air support against the other. These two units were to keep the Egyptians busy while the main body of Allon's forces moved south along an ancient Roman road and attacked from the rear. On December 26, they took the fortress at al-Auja and from there pressed deep into the Sinai Peninsula.

By December 29, the fighting had come to a standstill and the U.N. Security Council organized peace talks on the island of Rhodes. Dr. Ralph Bunche of the United States took over as mediator. Unlike the aristocratic Bernadotte, Bunche was a self-made man, an African-American who had worked his way through college and knew prejudice and hatred.

## The Armistice

With patience and considerable personal charm, Bunche eventually put together an armistice agreement between Israel and its Arab neighbors. None of them was

*Ralph Bunche assumed the position of U.N. mediator and negotiated a treaty between Israel, Egypt, and Jordan.*

The 1947–48 war was a watershed event in the history of Palestine's Arabs, as well as its Jews. The war's meaning for the two peoples was completely different, however. With their nationalist aspirations thwarted, the results filled Palestinians with despair, rather than with hope and anticipation. Indeed, Palestinians refer to the defeat of 1947–48 as ad-naqba, "the catastrophe" or "the disaster." [83]

By terms of the treaty, Israel kept the territories it had occupied during the war, giving it 77 percent of Palestine. Egypt controlled the Gaza Strip, and King Abdullah claimed the West Bank area of central Palestine for his renamed kingdom of Jordan. There was nothing left for an Arab state. The U.N. partition plan of 1947 was a dead issue, and the Palestinian Arabs had become landless refugees, adrift in a world that did not want them.

Their plight was largely ignored by the Israelis, who were struggling to transform their raw young state into a unique Jewish society. That task would prove to be far more difficult than most of them could have imagined.

delighted with the treaty, nor did they expect it to bring about a permanent peace. For the time being, however, they agreed to live with it. The Palestinian Arabs did not agree, as Mark Tessler described:

# 8 Becoming Israeli

From the earliest days of its nationhood, factionalism was a defining trait of Israeli life. People came to Israel from all over the world, speaking the languages and following customs of their former homes, sharing almost nothing beyond the fact of being Jewish and the predominant belief that they, and not the Arabs, had a right to the land.

## Laying the Foundations of Government

When Israel held its first elections on January 25, 1949, over twenty different political parties vied with one another for 120 seats in the first Knesset (Israeli parliament).

Multiple parties are a common feature of European-style parliamentary democracies. Because no one party can gain a majority, the government functions by building coalitions (alliances) behind a prime minister who comes from the strongest party in the coalition. When a coalition collapses, as sometimes happens during economic or political crisis, the prime minister must resign and call for a general election to empower a new government.

About 440,000 people voted in the first Israeli election. The left wing Labor-Socialist coalition won fifty-seven seats, the Center-Right-wing parties thirty-one, and the religious parties sixteen. As leader of the dominant party in the Labor-Socialist coalition, David Ben-Gurion became prime minister. Chaim Weizmann was chosen as president by unanimous vote of the first Knesset.

In a parliamentary democracy, the real power as head of state resides with the prime minister. The president serves a ceremonial function. After a lifetime of working for the Zionist cause, Weizmann, wrote Norman Rose, was not prepared for this kind of office:

> From the onset, Weizmann attempted to elicit some indication of the powers he would have and the role he would play as president. He was unwilling to be a mere figurehead. . . . But his enquiries were neatly stonewalled, and this increased his suspicions of what lay ahead. . . . [He] was told that the presidency was to be a symbol, but until his last days he claimed to be unable to fathom what this "vague statement" meant; in his heart, he knew.[84]

Loyal Zionist that he was, Chaim Weizmann would serve as president of Israel until his death on November 9, 1952, just a few days short of his seventy-eighth birthday.

*Chaim Weizmann (with hand raised) is sworn in as president of Israel on February 19, 1949. Weizmann was elected unanimously by the first Knesset.*

## Multiparty Problems

Ben-Gurion also had to deal with unwelcome limitations to his power. To preserve fragile coalitions in a multiparty system, he had to make concessions to minority members. Though Ben-Gurion himself favored an entirely secular government, he could not ignore the religious parties. They were determined that Orthodox (strictly religious) Judaism should play a major role in shaping the first Jewish state in nearly two thousand years.

They secured public observance of the Sabbath and other religious holidays. The Jewish Sabbath begins at sundown on Friday and continues until sundown Saturday. For those twenty-four hours, everything from stores and restaurants to banks and government agencies closes down.

Religious authorities also gained jurisdiction over laws and regulations dealing with personal status, meaning issues such as marriage, divorce, burial, and inheritance. Even nonobservant, secular Jews were answerable to rabbinical courts in these areas. Christians and Muslims were not. These minority faiths established their own religious courts to oversee personal status matters.

Israel's Orthodox minority was not content to be the sole Jewish authority in matters of religion. In their opinion, a Jewish state had to be governed by Jewish (religious) Law. Their struggle with the secular majority led to the first Knesset's failure to enact a formal constitution.

Ben-Gurion and his secularists had no intention of basing the founding document of their society on religious law. The religionists were equally determined that "only the Torah Law [the five biblical "books of Moses": Genesis, Exodus, Leviticus, Numbers, Deuteronomy] and tradition are sovereign in the life of Israel."[85]

Fortunately for the emerging nation, both sides realized that they could not write a constitution without addressing fundamental conflicts. "So they decided not to decide and were left without a constitution, but the 'Kulturkampf'[in German, cultural struggle] they had all feared was avoided."[86]

## The Ingathering of the Exiles

In the first eighteen months of Israel's existence as a nation, 350,000 Jews immigrated to the country. So many came so fast that the hard-pressed Israeli authorities had difficulty providing for them all. Despite the drain on scarce national resources, the Israelis believed that taking in immigrants was the essence of their national mission. In July 1950, the Knesset passed the Law of Return, which gave immediate citizenship to any Jewish immigrant who requested it.

While the Israelis were genuinely concerned for Holocaust survivors and other diaspora Jews who needed refuge, they were also eager to bring in strong, healthy people who would build new settlements. David Ben-Gurion regarded both immigration and pioneering settlement as essential to national security:

> Doubling and tripling the number of immigrants gives us more and more strength. . . . That is the most important thing. . . . We have conquered territories, but without settlements they have no decisive value, not in the Negev, nor in the Galilee, nor in Jerusalem. Settlement—that is the real conquest.[87]

The first priority of the government was to rescue the Holocaust survivors. They brought people from Germany, Austria, and Italy, and arranged exit visas for central European survivors who were in danger of being trapped behind the Iron Curtain of Soviet Communism.

The "Israeli Jews"—immigrants from the five alioth (plural of aliyah), and their children—were uncomfortable with the Holocaust survivors and their agonizing memories. Survivors represented diaspora Jews at their worst: downtrodden, victimized, set apart from the rest of humanity by generations of surviving on the edge of other people's cultures. Survivor Aviva Unger commented,

*Three Jewish children are on their way to Palestine after being released from Buchenwald concentration camp. Holocaust survivors were given top priority for immigration to Israel.*

The worst thing about coming here was the welcome. That I'd been in the Warsaw ghetto was a kind of scandal: no one wanted to talk about it. . . . On the surface, things were looked after; spiritually, there was no help at all.[88]

In addition to this group animosity, many Israelis found individual survivors strange and unlikable. Survivors, admitted Aviva Unger,

were quite different from normal people. People of my generation had their youth stolen, or their development arrested. In some ways you grew up fast, in others, not at all; thus I found myself here aged 26 with an eight-year-old daughter, but inside me, to all intents and purposes, I was still a 15-year-old girl. You have to have a very broad heart to understand someone like I was.[89]

## Immigration Problems

Even while Israel struggled to absorb Holocaust survivors, it was receiving thousands of immigrants who would be even harder to integrate: Jews from North Africa and the Levant (Eastern Mediterranean), often

---

### An Arab Confronts the Holocaust

*As Jews are capable of empathizing with the plight of dispossessed Arabs, so Arabs are capable of understanding the horrible impact of the Holocaust. In his book* Sleeping on a Wire: Conversations with Palestinians in Israel, *author David Grossman quotes Dr. Nazir Unes:*

"Last year I took an organized tour of Eastern Europe. The group included the children of Holocaust survivors, people whose families had been murdered there, people who themselves had been there, and partisan fighters. Obviously, the tour was centered round the extermination camps. I heard their stories, and they'd talk on the bus rides. . . . I went with some of them to look for their old houses. I took a cab with one member of the group and we went to his hometown, in Czechoslovakia. He remembered every street and every house. . . . In the extermination camps we visited I stood in front of the gas chambers. We lit candles, and all of a sudden everything you knew about the suffering and the history of the Jews runs through your head, and you tremble. . . . I asked a friend of mine, an Arab who was there with me, 'What does it mean to you that entire villages, whole towns were erased there in a single day?' and he answered me, 'What do you want, look what they're doing to us now.'"

---

*Operation Magic Carpet brought thousands of immigrant Jews from Yemen. Here, a small group from the airlift rescue sits by the plane after arriving in Israel.*

collectively called Orientals (literally, easterners). The strange customs and "primitiveness" of these people was a source of concern to Israeli officials. They came from Algeria and Morocco, Syria, Libya, and Iran. The most publicized group came from Yemen in Operation Magic Carpet, a massive airlift rescue that brought forty-nine thousand Yemenite Jews to Israel at a total cost of $4 million. Tom Segev, describing the Oriental Jews, wrote,

> Many could not read or write in any language. Many had received minimal education, often only a religious one. . . . They knew no Hebrew and were unfamiliar with the bureaucratic system. They brought with them a communal-patriarchal tradition which left little room for individual initiative.[90]

Members of the Knesset openly expressed concern about "preserving our cultural standards given the massive immigration from the Orient."[91] To avoid this cultural disintegration, the leadership agreed that "the immigrants from the Arab countries had to be uplifted from their backward state."[92]

Few questioned whether these immigrants would *want* to be "uplifted," but some did question whether they *could* be. In a controversial 1951 newspaper article, journalist Arye Gelblum concluded that the task was impossible: "The peculiar tragedy with these immigrants . . . is that there is nothing to hope for from their children, either. To raise their general standards . . . would take generations!"[93]

## "Golda's Cannons"

Despite the overwhelming problems, Israel's commitment to mass immigration did not waver. Immigration officials warned that they had no facilities for so many, but still the people came. New arrivals went to

## The Dangers of Stereotypes

"[Some] of the tensions between the Ashkenazi and Sephardi Jews in Israel can be attributed to the dynamics of prejudice against Arabs. The Ashkenazim are Jews with origins in Europe and North America; some of their fathers and grandfathers settled as the original Zionist pioneers in Palestine before the creation of the Jewish state. The Sephardim, a term initially applied to the Jews in Spain, now include those with origins mostly in the Muslim countries of North Africa and the Middle East. . . . Colloquially, they are also known as Oriental or Eastern Jews. . . . [One] of the leading stereotypes attached to the Sephardim is that they are primitive, tribal, crude—that there is something Arab about them. Their music is infused with the keyless quarter-tones of Arab music; their families are extended, and infatuated with elaborate tradition; their food is decidedly Middle Eastern. Much of their culture has been absorbed from the Arab countries in which they have lived. Many speak at least a mangled Arabic, and because they generally have black hair and olive skin, they bear a physical resemblance to the Arabs."

a reception center where immigration authorities checked their identity papers, customs officials inspected their luggage, and medical workers examined their bodies. This process was supposed to take a few days, but the system did not work efficiently. The new arrivals simply had no place to go, so they remained in the reception center, living in overcrowded tents without kitchens or sanitary facilities.

Hundreds, even thousands, of bewildered immigrants crowded into these facilities, entirely dependent upon the government for their daily subsistence.

Adults did not go to work because there was no work; children did not go to school because there was no school. Hundreds sickened and died because there was no medical care. A few thousand immigrants found housing in abandoned Arab villages, and some joined existing kibbutzim, but most stayed in the camps, doubtlessly wondering if coming to Israel had been the mistake of their lives.

The job of housing these immigrants fell to the Ministry of Labor, directed at the time by Golda Meir. This Russian-born schoolteacher from Milwaukee, Wisconsin, had joined an aliyah in 1921. She prided herself on being a hard-nosed realist with a talent for recognizing what is essential and what is not. In the spring of 1949, she announced a program to mass produce housing. Most of these units would be cottages of concrete blocks, made on the spot by long-barreled casting machines—"Golda's cannons," people called them.

Some members of the Knesset objected to this starkly utilitarian housing, but Meir had a ready answer for them: the plan would work because it had to work. To her, it really was that simple:

> There is no harm if a family of three, or even of four, lived in one single room. We intend to provide a roof. Not a ceiling—a roof. No plaster—only whitewash. The immigrant himself will in time plaster the walls and add a ceiling. A few months later he will add a room and a porch.[94]

By the end of the year, Golda's cannons had made twenty-five thousand of these houses. That was far from enough to fill the growing need, so the government also created new and better immigrant settlements called maabaroth (transit camps). Each family had a tent of its own, though the water supply and sanitary facilities were still communal. Most important of all, the maabaroth were near population centers where adults could find jobs and begin to establish connections with normal Israeli society.

In addition to finding work in the local economy, maabaroth residents were encouraged to elect their own councils, form clubs and associations, and generally make life in the maabaroth more bearable. The government established makeshift schools for the children, so they would not fall too far behind in their studies.

Even with these changes, there was terrible hardship among the newcomers. Inevitably, some of them were beaten down by the grim realities of their lives. By 1953, nearly forty thousand immigrants had left the country, giving up the dream of a homeland in Israel for the reality of a haven in western Europe or the Americas.

Those who stayed—and increasingly, those who came—were the Oriental Jews. In 1948, they had accounted for only 14 percent of total immigration. By 1953, fully 75 percent of new immigrants came from North Africa and the Levant, and the figure went up from there. According to Howard Sachar in his history of Israel,

> This constituted an ethnic revolution for the Zionist state, one that none of

*Golda Meir, director of the Ministry of Labor, initiated a housing project to provide immediate, basic shelter to the thousands of new Israeli immigrants.*

its leaders had anticipated, even after the Holocaust, nor as late as 1948. Far from serving as an outpost of the West in Asia, Israel itself appeared to be undergoing orientalization, both in human resources and to some degree in its way of life.[95]

## Manners and Mores

From its beginning, Israel struggled with layers of contradiction and conflict: pioneers against a harsh land, Jews against Arabs, Western Jews against Eastern Jews, secular Jews against religious Jews, left-wing Jews against right-wing Jews, and

Holocaust survivors against their own grim memories. Many times, these conflicts seemed on the verge of destroying the young nation.

Threats from the outside kept Israel together, uniting the squabbling factions by giving them a common enemy. Unlike their forebears in the diaspora, Israelis considered themselves pioneers and warriors. Their role models were kibbutzniks, soldiers, and sabras (native Israelis).

Sabras are named for a fruit that grows on a native variety of cactus. It is hard and prickly on the outside, incredibly sweet within. American journalist Harry Golden wrote:

As a fruit, the sabra is more trouble than it is worth. You cannot buy it in

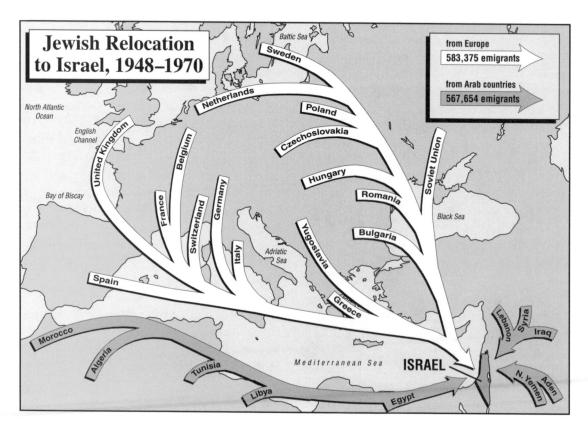

## The Cult of Toughness

*In* The Israelis: Founders and Sons, *Amos Elon observes how years of military preparedness have affected the younger generation of Israelis:*

"The first thing to note is a spreading cult of toughness. . . . A spartan rigidity has developed over the years and now marks large segments of the younger adult population. It often spills over from the military life, where it was acquired, to the civilian sphere. . . . The language of younger Israelis is often inordinately stark, divested of all ornament and elegance, without nuance, and delivered in harsh staccato sequences. One reason is that 'official' Hebrew is still too formal and lags far behind the needs of daily [life]: the developing street [slang] that substitutes for what is missing in the dictionary is still raw and unformed. Another reason may be more important. The harsh starkness that marks *sabra* speech and manners stems from many years of deliberate educational efforts to produce 'normal,' 'manly,' 'free,' 'new' Jews, unsullied by the shameful weaknesses of exile."

fruit stores nor are you served it in restaurants. Along the roads now and then you see little kids with a tin pail at the end of a long pole, trying to dislodge the sabra from the cactus. But as a symbol, the sabra is something else again. There is a sabra generation, a sabra vote, and a sabra [lifestyle]. It is something in Israel to be a sabra.[96]

Israelis tend to be blunt to the point of rudeness, with little patience for European ideas of social refinement. "They're a pioneer society," said American social worker Joseph Jacobs, during a 1973 visit to Israeli social service agencies. "I doubt if refinement was very important in Dodge City or Deadwood, either."[97]

Many Israelis would like that comparison to the rough-and-ready frontier spirit of the American West. Others would not have liked it at all. Immigrants from prosperous, well-educated backgrounds could not help missing the refinement and social graces they had learned as children. Aviva Unger, a Holocaust survivor, commented,

As I get older, I go more and more frequently to Europe. I think I still have a sense of roots there, which I cannot be rid of. I am European and I am not European. My daughter and son-in-law lived in Hampstead [England] for many years before coming out here. One of the things that made me feel quite sad was seeing my grandson

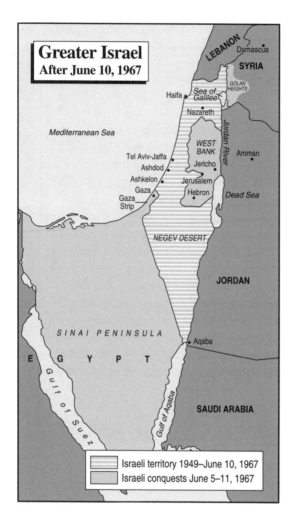

**Greater Israel**
**After June 10, 1967**

LEBANON
Damascus
SYRIA
GOLAN HEIGHTS
Haifa
Sea of Galilee
Nazareth
Mediterranean Sea
Jordan River
WEST BANK
Amman
Tel Aviv-Jaffa
Ashdod
Jericho
Ashkelon
Jerusalem
Gaza
Hebron
Dead Sea
Gaza Strip
NEGEV DESERT
JORDAN
SINAI PENINSULA
Aqaba
E G Y P T
Gulf of Suez
Gulf of Aqaba
SAUDI ARABIA

Israeli territory 1949–June 10, 1967
Israeli conquests June 5–11, 1967

Holocaust survivor Feliciya Karay, who grew up in Krakow, Poland, echoed Unger's sentiments:

> I've never regretted coming here. I'll tell you frankly, too, that I love to go back to Europe, because the weather and the landscape remind me of childhood, but I would never go back there to live. I am very patriotic. Very patriotic. I know there is a lot wrong here, but it is *our* country.[100]

## Hero Journeys

The career of Moshe Dayan in many ways parallels the military and social development of his country. He was the very embodiment of the Israeli ideal: a kibbutz-born sabra with a distinguished military record. It seemed the most natural thing in the world for the famed "one-eyed general" to become army chief of staff in December 1953. Within two years, he reorganized the army and transformed its small size from a liability into an asset.

The process started with the officer corps. In other armies, officers directed the battle from the rear. Moshe Dayan personally led his troops into combat, and insisted that all his officers do the same. Officers lead, they do not point, he said. He made it a standing order.

Dayan could not build a large army, so he created a streamlined fighting unit that did not need a vast network of support units in the field. Israeli forces could move swiftly, strike fiercely, and inflict maximum damage on the enemy in the shortest possible time.

Israel's army defeated the Egyptians in the Sinai Campaign of 1956. Just over ten years later, in June 1967, Israeli forces took

change from being a polite little English schoolboy into a rude little Israeli.[98]

Like Aviva Unger, many immigrants are not entirely comfortable with the rough-edged Israeli image; nonetheless, they still love their country. Unger herself reflected that

> it is Israel that gave me back my pride, allowed me to develop my career, provided a home for my family. . . . My argument turns back on itself. I don't belong to Europe, and I probably do belong here.[99]

the West Bank and the old city of Jerusalem from Jordan, most of the Sinai Peninsula from Egypt, and the Golan Heights from Syria. This was the famous Six Day War, which quickly became a legend of modern warfare.

Moshe Dayan became a legend as well. Children put on black eye patches in imitation of him, musicians wrote ballads, stand-up comics told stories that added to his legend.

He seemed invincible, superhuman—until a surprise attack on October 6, 1973, caught Israeli forces off guard. It was Yom Kippur, the Day of Atonement, holiest day of the Jewish year. Nobody expected a war. Then Syria attacked from the north, and Egypt from the south. They caused heavy damages before Dayan could rally his troops and regain most of the territory that had been lost.

After the shooting stopped, the Israeli people realized that Dayan was mortal, fallible—and that they were, too. The Yom Kippur War was a pivotal moment for the entire nation. Dayan stepped down as chief of staff and defense minister. Golda Meir, who was by this time prime minister, resigned after failing to build a coalition strong enough to govern the country.

Israel endured. Surrounded by enemies, weakened by factionalism, often falling short of its founding ideals, it endured. In the twenty-first century, endurance will not be enough.

# The Ongoing Challenge

On May 14, 1998, the reborn Jewish state observes its fiftieth anniversary. The years since the Yom Kippur War have put both its principles and its people to the test.

Many surprises occurred along the way, such as the election of 1977, which broke the Labor Party government of Prime Minister Yitzhak Rabin. The hard-line Likud Party gained enough seats in the Knesset to form a new coalition government, headed by former Irgun commander Menachem Begin.

## Prime Minister Menachem Begin

The fiery young revolutionary who once ran naval blockades and defied the British mandate became one of the architects of the famous Camp David Accords, the agreement that was to become the foundation of future peace negotiations. On September 17, 1979, at Camp David, Maryland, Begin and Egyptian president Anwar Sadat signed the Accords.

The agreement made international news; all the wire services carried a photo of the two leaders shaking hands, while U.S. president Jimmy Carter looked on, smiling. The following November, Begin and Sadat shared the Nobel Peace Prize for their historic achievement.

*Menachem Begin speaks to Jewish organizations in New York in 1979. The same year, Begin signed the Camp David Accords with Anwar Sadat and won the Nobel Peace Prize.*

Two-and-a-half years later, on October 6, 1981, Anwar Sadat was assassinated by an Islamic extremist. His former "partner in peace," Menachem Begin, was leading Israel toward a costly war in Lebanon.

In the early 1980s, Lebanon became a base of Arab guerrilla activity. Under the leadership of Yasser Arafat, the Palestine Liberation Organization (PLO) operated in refugee camps, where displaced Palestinians still dreamed of going home to land now claimed by Israel.

From its bases in Lebanon, the PLO was able to shell Israeli settlements in the Upper Galilee. To the Israelis, this was an intolerable situation. On June 5, 1982, Prime Minister Begin called an emergency cabinet meeting. At the recommendation of Defense Minister Ariel Sharon, Israel prepared to mount a limited military operation into Lebanon. The objective was to clear a twenty-five-mile strip, driving PLO artillery out of range of Israel's northern settlements.

On June 6, 1982, eighty thousand troops under command of General Rafael Eytan began an assault to encircle and destroy the Palestinian forces. Operation Peace for the Galilee, as it was called, lasted from June 6–11, 1982, but that proved to be only the beginning.

## Shamir and Peres

The "limited" attack turned into an invasion, and the invasion into an occupation. Hostilities stretched out, multiplying casualties on both sides, solving nothing. By September 1983, the ill-fated adventure left the Middle East political situation more tangled than ever, shook Israel's

*Menachem Begin resigned as prime minister of Israel in 1983.*

faith in its military leaders, and led to Begin's resignation.

The action in Lebanon also depleted the national treasury, contributing to an inflation rate of nearly 400 percent. On September 15, 1983, Likud hard-liner Yitzhak Shamir became prime minister—just in time to preside over the worst economic crisis in national history. The value of Israel's currency plunged and banks floundered. The government poured funds into the banks, saving them from failure, and provided $150 million to save the stock exchange from total collapse.

In addition to these potential disasters, the already-huge defense budget was strained to the breaking point by the Israeli occupation of Lebanon. Frightened Israelis began to look for a change in government. In September 1984, a new Labor alignment broke the Likud majority in the Knesset. They did not, however, have sufficient seats to form a ruling coalition.

The result was a strange form of shared power between Likud and Labor. Shimon Peres of the Labor Party would become prime minister for twenty-five months, with Shamir as foreign minister. At the end of that period, the positions would reverse, with Shamir assuming the prime ministry, and Peres stepping down to foreign minister.

Under Peres, Israeli troops finally withdrew from their positions in Lebanon. By June 1985, most of the soldiers were home, ending three years of occupation that had cost Israel 654 dead, 3,873 wounded, and $5 billion (U.S.) in expenditures.

Military adventurism, economic difficulties, and lack of stability in government damaged Israel's standing among the nations of the world. As right-wing nationalists and ultra-Orthodox religionists became more strident in their demands, moderate Israelis voiced concern.

Shulamit Aloni, leader of the Citizens' Rights Party, warned that "Israel is being converted from a democratic, humanistic state to an Orthodox, clerical community. . . . Laws with racist and discriminatory overtones are beginning to find their way onto the books."[101]

During the 1991 Gulf War, Prime Minister Yitzhak Shamir cooperated with the United States by taking no independent action against Iraq. At the same time, he was asking for $10 billion in American loan guarantees. The outcome of that request was a rude awakening for Shamir's government. Though President George Bush approved a short-term grant to repair war damage in Tel Aviv, he refused to authorize the $10 billion unless Israel

*A kibbutznik hoists the flag. Though a young nation, Israel grapples with ancient strife.*

halted settlement of the West Bank, a region claimed by both Arabs and Jews.

The hard-line Shamir would not budge on his territorial expansion policies, but many Israelis felt differently. They were growing tired of the endless killing, the terrorism, and the warfare. In the election of June 23, 1992, they handed Likud and its right-wing coalition partners a decisive defeat at the polls.

## A Battle for Peace

For the second time in his career, Yitzhak Rabin became prime minister. He had promised a government dedicated to the search for a negotiated peace, and he kept his word. On September 13, 1993, Rabin and PLO leader Yasser Arafat signed a Declaration of Principles that would lead to Palestinian self-government on the West Bank. The next day, Rabin met with Jordan's King Hussein to sign a similar pact, setting forth principles to normalize relations between the two old enemies. In a stirring tribute to the peace, Yitzhak Rabin spoke after the signing: "I, who served my country for twenty-seven years as a soldier, I say to you . . . this is the only battle that is a pleasure to win: the battle for peace. . . . God bless the peace."[102]

Not everyone shared these sentiments. Extremists on both sides engaged in acts of terrorism, attempting to stall the peace process. On November 4, 1995, a twenty-five-year-old Israeli law student named Yigal Amir assassinated Yitzhak Rabin for the "crime" of seeking a peaceful solution to the long nightmare of the Middle East.

Following that assassination, terrorism increased on both sides, and peace talks between Israel and the PLO stalled. In May 1996, the Israeli people seemed to turn from Rabin's vision when they elected a Likud government, headed by the hawkish but charismatic Benjamin Netanyahu.

The fate of the Middle East peace process, and of Israel itself, remains to be seen. To thrive as a nation, Israel must solve many problems. How it deals with its neighbors, its Arab minority, and its own identity crisis will ultimately determine how history judges this contentious, imperfect little nation that started with a dream.

# Notes

### Introduction: Revival in an Ancient Land

1. Quoted in "1940s Highlights—State of Israel," *Time Almanac Reference Edition* (CD-ROM). Washington, DC: Compact Publishing, 1994.

2. Quoted in Norman Rose, *Chaim Weizmann*. New York: Viking Press, 1986, p. 433.

### Chapter 1: A People Dispossessed

3. Quoted in Robert Chazan, *In the Year 1096 . . . The First Crusade and the Jews.* Philadelphia: Jewish Publication Society, 1996, p. 3.

4. Nathan Ausubel, *The Book of Jewish Knowledge.* New York: Crown Publishers, 1964, p. 498.

5. Fourth Lateran Council, *Church Laws Concerning Jews,* quoted in Alexis P. Rubin, ed., *Scattered Among the Nations: Documents Affecting Jewish History 49 to 1975.* Northvale, NJ: Jason Aronson, 1995, p. 52.

6. Edict of Louis IX, quoted in Ausubel, *The Book of Jewish Knowledge,* p. 498.

7. Ausubel, *The Book of Jewish Knowledge,* pp. 298–99.

8. Ausubel, *The Book of Jewish Knowledge,* p. 342.

9. Ausubel, *The Book of Jewish Knowledge,* p. 342.

10. Ausubel, *The Book of Jewish Knowledge,* p. 344.

11. Rubin, *Scattered Among the Nations,* p. 160.

### Chapter 2: Theodore Herzl and the Zionist Ideal

12. Chaim Potok, *Wanderings: Chaim Potok's History of the Jews.* New York: Fawcett Crest Books, 1980, p. 519.

13. Mark Tessler, *A History of the Israeli-Palestinian Conflict.* Bloomington: Indiana University Press, 1994, p. 59.

14. Alex Bein, *Theodore Herzl: A Biography.* Translated by Maurice Samuel. London: East and West Library, 1956, p. 176.

15. Bein, *Theodore Herzl,* p. 179.

16. Quoted in Bein, *Theodore Herzl,* pp. 115–16.

17. Quoted in Bein, *Theodore Herzl,* p. 128.

18. Baron Moritz de Hirsch, quoted in Bein, *Theodore Herzl,* p. 128.

19. Theodore Herzl, quoted in Howard M. Sachar, *A History of Israel: From the Rise of Zionism to Our Time,* 2nd ed. New York: Alfred A. Knopf, 1996, p. 38.

20. Bein, *Theodore Herzl,* p. 140.

21. Max Nordau, quoted in Sachar, *A History of Israel,* p. 39.

22. Stefan Zweig, quoted in Sachar, *A History of Israel,* p. 42.

23. Chaim Weizmann, *Trial and Error.* 1949. Reprint, New York: Greenwood Publishing Group, 1972, p. 61.

### Chapter 3: Founders and Pioneers

24. Quoted in Leo Trepp, *The Complete Book of Jewish Observance: A Practical Manual for the Modern Jew.* New York: Behrman House, 1980, p. 24.

25. Quoted in Bein, *Theodore Herzl,* p. 243.

26. Quoted in Sachar, *A History of Israel,* pp. 50–51.

27. Quoted in Sachar, *A History of Israel,* p. 61.

28. Rose, *Chaim Weizmann,* p. 70.

29. Rose, *Chaim Weizmann,* p. 73.

30. Weizmann, *Trial and Error,* p. 114.

31. Tessler, *A History of the Israeli-Palestinian Conflict,* p. 145.

32. Rose, *Chaim Weizmann,* p. 183.

33. Rose, *Chaim Weizmann,* p. 182.

### Chapter 4: Between Two Wars

34. Celia S. Heller, *On the Edge of Destruction: Jews of Poland Between the Two World Wars.* New York: Schocken Books, 1980, pp. 267–68.

35. Golda Meir, quoted in Ralph G. Martin, *Golda Meir: The Romantic Years*. New York: Charles Scribner's Sons, 1988, p. 111.

36. Rose, Chaim Weizmann, p. 103.

37. Quoted in Rose, *Chaim Weizmann*, p. 229.

38. Tom Segev, *The Seventh Million: The Israelis and the Holocaust*. New York: Hill and Wang, 1993, p. 35.

39. Segev, *The Seventh Million*, pp. 52-53.

40. Quoted in Sachar, *A History of Israel*, p. 199.

41. David Ben-Gurion, quoted in Segev, *The Seventh Million*, p. 83.

### Chapter 5: No Man's Land

42. Segev, *The Seventh Million*, p. 82.

43. Rose, *Chaim Weizmann*, p. 387.

44. Tessler, *A History of the Israeli-Palestinian Conflict*, p. 250.

45. Walter Laqueur and Barry Rubin, eds., *The Israeli-Arab Reader: A Documentary History of the Middle East Conflict*. New York: Penguin Books, 1984, pp. 77-79.

46. Quoted in Rose, *Chaim Weizmann*, p. 379.

47. J. C. Hurewitz, *The Struggle for Palestine*. New York: Schocken Books, 1976, p. 195.

48. Peter Hay, *Ordinary Heroes: The Life and Death of Chana Szenes, Israel's National Heroine*. New York: Paragon House, 1989, p. 138.

49. Hay, *Ordinary Heroes*, p. 3.

50. Hay, *Ordinary Heroes*, p. 183.

51. Segev, *The Seventh Million*, p. 472.

52. Rose, *Chaim Weizmann*, p. 395.

53. Winston Churchill, quoted in Rose, *Chaim Weizmann*, p. 396.

54. Quoted in Rose, *Chaim Weizmann*, p. 399.

55. Quoted in Rose, *Chaim Weizmann*, p. 402.

### Chapter 6: Fighting for the Dream

56. Francesca M. Wilson, *Aftermath: France, Germany, Austria, Yugoslavia, 1945 & 1946*. London: Penguin Books, 1947, pp. 40–41.

57. Quoted in Sachar, *A History of Israel*, p. 251.

58. David McCullough, *Truman*. New York: Simon and Schuster, 1992, pp. 595–96.

59. Azzam Pasha, quoted in Rose, *Chaim Weizmann*, p. 259.

60. Richard Crossman, quoted in Rose, *Chaim Weizmann*, p. 408.

61. McCullough, *Truman*, p. 600.

62. Rose, *Chaim Weizmann*, p. 407.

63. Quoted in Sachar, *A History of Israel*, p. 265.

64. Keren Markuze, "The Bomb That Triggered Independence," *Jerusalem Post*, July 22, 1996, p. 7.

65. Markuze, "The Bomb That Triggered Independence," p. 7.

66. Sachar, *A History of Israel*, p. 267.

67. Segev, *The Seventh Million*, p. 130.

68. Segev, *The Seventh Million*, p. 131.

69. Segev, *The Seventh Million*, p. 132.

70. Michele Chabin, "Exodus Survivors Want Truth Told," *USA Today*, May 19, 1997, p. 16A.

71. Quoted in Chabin, "Exodus Survivors Want Truth Told," p. 16.

72. Quoted in Tessler, *A History of the Israeli-Palestinian Conflict*, p. 261.

73. Tom Segev, *1949: The First Israelis*. New York: Free Press, 1986, p. 25n.

74. Benny Morris, *The Birth of the Palestinian Refugee Problem, 1947–1949*. Cambridge, England: Cambridge University Press, 1987, pp. 113–14.

75. Menachem Begin, *The Revolt: Story of the Irgun*. New York: Henry Schuman, 1951, p. 228.

### Chapter 7: Building a Nation

76. Quoted in Rose, *Chaim Weizmann*, p. 440.

77. Quoted in "1940s Highlights—May 24, 1948," *Time Almanac Reference Edition* CD-ROM.

78. Quoted in Sachar, *A History of Israel*, p. 315.

79. Sachar, *A History of Israel*, p. 329.

80. Sachar, *A History of Israel*, p. 329.

81. Seth Lipsky, "When the Ship of State Floundered: New Documentary Recalls the Civil War That Almost Was." Stamford, CT: Ethnic NewsWatch, SoftLine Information, Inc., Dec. 2, 1994, pp. PG.

82. Quoted in Lipsky, "When the Ship of State Floundered," n.p.

83. Tessler, *A History of the Israeli-Palestinian Conflict,* p. 273.

### Chapter 8: Becoming Israeli

84. Rose, *Chaim Weizmann,* p. 445.

85. Rabbi I. M. Levin, quoted in Segev, *1949,* p. 262.

86. Segev, *1949,* p. 262.

87. Quoted in Segev, *1949,* p. 97.

88. Aviva Unger, quoted in Anton Gill, *The Journey Back from Hell: Conversations with Concentration Camp Survivors.* New York: William Morrow and Co., 1988, p. 281.

89. Quoted in Gill, *The Journey Back from Hell,* p. 281.

90. Segev, *1949,* p. 171.

91. Segev, *1949,* p. 156.

92. Segev, *1949,* p. 158.

93. Arye Gelblum, "Haaretz," March 22, 1951, quoted in Segev, *1949,* p. 161.

94. Golda Meir, quoted in Segev, *1949,* p. 133.

95. Sachar, *A History of Israel,* p. 403.

96. Harry Golden, *The Israelis: Portrait of a People.* New York: G. P. Putnam's Sons, 1971, p. 23.

97. Conversation with the author, 10/73.

98. Quoted in Gill, *The Journey Back from Hell,* p. 282.

99. Quoted in Gill, *The Journey Back from Hell,* p. 282.

100. Quoted in Gill, *The Journey Back from Hell,* p. 275.

### Epilogue: The Ongoing Challenge

101. Shulamit Aloni, quoted in Sachar, *A History of Israel,* p. 926.

102. Yitzhak Rabin, quoted in Sachar, *A History of Israel,* p. 1,001.

# For Further Reading

David Bamberger, *Young Person's History of Israel*. New York: Behrman House, 1985. A basic overview of the events leading up to Israeli statehood.

Lawrence J. Epstein, ed., *A Treasury of Jewish Inspirational Stories*. Northvale, NJ: Jason Aronson, 1993. A collection of writings on Israel and other Jewish topics.

Harry Golden, *The Israelis: Portrait of a People*. New York: G. P. Putnam's Sons, 1971. A warm, often humorous, look at the Israeli people.

Peter Hay, *Ordinary Heroes: The Life and Death of Chana Szenes, Israel's National Heroine*. New York: Paragon House, 1989. Biography of the kibbutznik who gave her life attempting to save Hungarian Jews from the Nazis.

Peter Hellman, *Heroes: Tales from the Israeli Wars*. New York: Henry Holt, 1990. Collective biography of ordinary Israeli soldiers.

Carol Matas, *The Garden*. New York: Simon and Schuster, 1997. Historically accurate fiction about a young girl who joins Haganah in the days before Israeli statehood.

# Works Consulted

Nathan Ausubel, *The Book of Jewish Knowledge.* New York: Crown Publishers, 1964. An encyclopedic listing of Jewish history, culture, and religion.

Menachem Begin, *The Revolt: Story of the Irgun.* New York: Henry Schuman, 1951. Begin's autobiographical account of Irgun activities in the struggle for independence.

Alex Bein, *Theodore Herzl: A Biography.* Translated by Maurice Samuel. London: East and West Library, 1956. A thorough treatment of the life of the Zionist pioneer.

Michele Chabin, "Exodus Survivors Want Truth Told," *USA Today,* May 19, 1997. Article about discrepancies between the actual *Exodus* voyage, and the movie version.

Robert Chazan, *In the Year 1096 . . . The First Crusade and the Jews.* Philadelphia: Jewish Publication Society, 1996. A scholarly history of violence against Jews in Christian Europe.

Albert Einstein, *Ideas and Opinions.* New York: Bonanza Books, 1954. A collection of writings, speeches, and letters from the great physicist.

Amos Elon, *The Israelis: Founders and Sons.* New York: Holt, Rinehart and Winston, 1971. The distinguished Israeli novelist looks at the first generations of Israelis.

Anton Gill, *The Journey Back from Hell: Conversations with Concentration Camp Survivors.* New York: William Morrow and Co., 1988. How survivors adjusted after the war; includes case histories of survivors who settled in Israel.

David Grossman, *Sleeping on a Wire: Conversations with Palestinians in Israel.* Translated by Haim Watzman, New York: Farrar, Straus and Giroux, 1993. A sensitive study of the Palestinian problem through Arab eyes.

Celia S. Heller, *On the Edge of Destruction: Jews of Poland Between the Two World Wars.* New York: Schocken Books, 1980. A social history of Polish Jewry and Polish Zionism.

J. C. Hurewitz, *The Struggle for Palestine.* New York: Schocken Books, 1976. A history of the military and diplomatic issues involved in the Palestinian question.

Walter Laqueur and Barry Rubin, eds., *The Israeli-Arab Reader: A Documentary History of the Middle East Conflict.* New York: Penguin Books, 1984. Primary source documents relating to Middle Eastern issues.

Bernard Lazare, *Antisemitism: Its History and Causes.* 1894. Reprinted, Lincoln: University of Nebraska Press, 1995. A nineteenth-century Jewish journalist explores and explains anti-Semitism in history.

Seth Lipsky, "When the Ship of State Floundered: New Documentary Recalls the Civil War That Almost Was." Stamford, CT: Ethnic NewsWatch, Soft-Line Information, Inc., Dec. 2, 1993. Article on the *Altalena* conflict that pitted Haganah against Irgun.

Keren Markuze, "The Bomb That Triggered Independence," *Jerusalem Post,* July 22, 1996. Discusses the bombing of the King David Hotel.

Ralph G. Martin, *Golda Meir: The Romantic Years.* New York: Charles Scribner's

Sons, 1988. A biography of Meir, concentrating on her younger years.

David McCullough, *Truman*. New York: Simon and Schuster. 1992. The life of the president who dealt with Chaim Weizmann.

Benny Morris, *The Birth of the Palestinian Refugee Problem, 1947–1949*. Cambridge, England: Cambridge University Press, 1987. A detailed look at the origins and consequences of Arab flight from Israeli Palestine.

Chaim Potok, *Wanderings: Chaim Potok's History of the Jews*. New York: Fawcett Crest Books, 1980. A history of the Jewish people from antiquity to modern times.

Bernard S. Raskas, *Heart of Wisdom Book III*. New York: United Commission on Jewish Education, 1986. A look at the Jewish people through a collection of anecdotes, sayings, and tales.

Norman Rose, *Chaim Weizmann*. New York: Viking Books, 1986. The definitive biography of the Zionist leader.

Alexis P. Rubin, ed., *Scattered Among the Nations: Documents Affecting Jewish History 49 to 1975*. Northvale, NJ: Jason Aronson, 1995. Anthology of documents from Jewish and non-Jewish sources.

Danny Rubinstein, *The People of Nowhere: The Palestinian Vision of Home*. Translated by Ina Freidman. New York: Random House, 1991. A moving look at Israel's refugee problem from the Palestinian point of view.

Howard M. Sachar, *A History of Israel: From the Rise of Zionism to Our Time*, 2nd. ed. New York: Alfred A. Knopf, 1996. A thorough history of nineteenth- and twentieth-century Israel.

Tom Segev, *1949: The First Israelis*. New York: Free Press, 1986. A hard-hitting study of Israel's early struggles to define itself.

Tom Segev, *The Seventh Million: The Israelis and the Holocaust*. New York: Hill and Wang, 1993. A close look at Israel's difficult absorption of Holocaust survivors.

David K. Shipler, *Arab and Jew: Wounded Spirits in a Promised Land*. New York: Penguin Books, 1986. A study of central issues from both viewpoints.

Christopher Simpson, *The Splendid Blond Beast: Money, Law, and Genocide in the Twentieth Century*. New York: Grove Press, 1993. A study of twentieth-century genocide and its effects on society.

Mark Tessler, *A History of the Israeli-Palestinian Conflict*. Bloomington: Indiana University Press, 1994. A detailed, cross-cultural history of the problem.

*Time Almanac Reference Edition* (CD-ROM). Washington, DC: Compact Publishing, 1994.

Leo Trepp, *The Complete Book of Jewish Observance: A Practical Manual for the Modern Jew*. New York: Behrman House, 1980. A basic guide to Jewish religious practices, including transliterated (English spelling of Hebrew words) prayers and instructions for observance.

Chaim Weizmann, *Trial and Error*. 1949. Reprint, New York: Greenwood Publishing Group, 1972. Weizmann's autobiography.

Francesca M. Wilson, *Aftermath: France, Germany, Austria, Yugoslavia, 1945 & 1946*. London: Penguin Books, 1947. An excellent look at the immediate postwar issues.

*Zionism: A Basic Reader*. New York: Herzl Press, 1975. An anthology of writings on Zionism.

# Index

Abdullah (king of
   Transjordan), 82, 84
"Address to the Rothschilds,
   An" (Herzl), 30
Ahad Ha'am, 27, 34–35
Alexander I (czar of Russia),
   19
Alexander III (czar of
   Russia), 20
aliyah (immigration)
   first, 24
   second, 39
   third, 42
   fourth, 42, 45
   fifth, 47
Allied powers, 52
Allon, Yigal, 83
*Altalena*, 79–80
Amir, Yigal, 99
Anglo-American Committee
   of Inquiry, 65–67
anti-Semitism
   of Adolf Hitler, 11, 47
   Dreyfus affair and, 28, 29
   in France, 26
   origins of term, 21
   in Russia, 25
*Antisemitism: Its History and
   Causes* (Lazare), 25
Arab Higher Committee, 72
Arab invasion of Palestine,
   map of, 81
Arab-Israeli conflicts
   after Bernadotte's death,
      83
   under British rule, 45
   emotional reasons for,
      50–51
   after fifth aliyah, 47–49
   investigated by Anglo-
      American Committee,
      65–67
   during 1948 War of
      Independence, 74, 76–79
   after Resolution 181, 72–73
   Weizmann's opinions on,
      11–12
   *see also* wars
Arab-Jewish conflict. *See* Arab-

Israeli conflicts
Arab Jews, 90
Arabs
   empathize with Holocaust
      survivors, 88
   flee Palestine after Deir
      Yassin, 73
   in Palestine during World
      War I, 40–41
   reaction to Anglo-
      American Committee
      report, 66
   reaction to Resolution 181,
      72
   suffer from Zionist
      progress, 43–44
Arafat, Yasir, 97, 99
armistice agreement, 83–84
Aryans, 21
Attlee, Clement, 65
*Auto-Emancipation* (Pinsker),
   26
Axis powers, 52

Baal Shem Tov, 18
badges, worn by Jews, 15
Balfour, Sir Arthur, 41
Balfour Declaration, 41, 49,
   52
baptism, Christian, Jews
   pressured into, 15, 17–18
Basle Program, 33, 34
Begin, Menachem
   elected prime minister, 96
   resigns, 97
   role in *Altalena* affair,
      79–81
   theories about Deir Yassin,
      73
   violent nature of, 68
Ben-Gurion, David, 52
   attempts release of D.P.
      camp victims, 64
   becomes prime minister,
      85
   conflicts with Weizmann,
      56–57
   declares independence for
      Israel, 74

handles government
      conflicts, 86–87
   reaction to "Black
      Sabbath," 68
   reaction to Irgun terrorism,
      68
   role in *Altalena* affair,
      79–80
   role in "trucks-for-blood"
      affair, 60
Ben Yehuda, Eliezer, 40, 50
Bernadotte, Count Folke, 79,
   82–83
Betar, 43
Bevin, Ernest, 67
Biltmore Program, 55–56, 57
Black Death, 16
"Black Sabbath," 67–68
blood libel, 14–15
Boleslav (king of Poland), 17
Brand, Hanzi, 61
Brand, Joel, 60–61
Brandeis, Louis D., 44
British government
   ends rule in Palestine, 72
   Jerusalem headquarters
      attacked, 68
   limits Jewish immigration
      to Palestine, 49, 52, 55, 67
   places Palestine under
      martial law, 68–69
   reaction to Anglo-
      American Committee
      report, 66–67
   reaction to *Exodus* affair,
      70–71
   retaliates after "Night of
      the Bridges," 67–68
Bunche, Ralph, 83–84
Bush, George, 98

Camp David Accords, 96
Carter, Jimmy, 96
Casimir III (king of Poland),
   17
Catherine the Great, 19
cease-fire of 1948, 79
chalutzim (pioneers), 38,
   39–40

Chamberlain, Joseph, 36
Chasidim (pious ones), 18–19
Chevrat Ovdim (Workers
    Association), 45
Chmielnicki, Bogdan, 18
Christian, Paul, 15, 18
Christians, efforts to convert
    Jews, 13–15, 20, 22
Churchill, Winston, 61, 62
Clement VI (pope), 16
cossacks, 18
Crusades, 13–14

Dayan, Moshe
    reorganizes Israeli army,
        94–95
    resigns, 95
    in Ten Days War, 82
    unorthodox tactics used by,
        78
death squads, Nazi
    (Einsatzkommandos), 56
Declaration of Independence
    (Israeli), 74
Declaration of Principles, 99
Deir Yassin, massacre at,
    72–73
diaspora, 13
Displaced Persons (D.P.)
    camps, 63–64
Dreyfus, Alfred, 28, 29

Eichmann, Adolf, 60
Einsatzkommandos (death
    squads), 56
Einstein, Albert, 32, 54
emancipation of Jews, 21–22
"Essay on the Inequality of
    the Human Races" (de
    Godineau), 21
"Eternal People, The"
    (Smolenskin), 24
Exodus (ship), 69–71

Fighters for Israel's Freedom.
    See Lehi
First Zionist Congress, 33–34
France, anti-Semitism in, 26

Ginzberg, Asher, 27
Gobineau, Arthur de, 21
"Golda's cannons," 91
Greenberg, Leopold, 36
Gulf War, 98

Haganah, 45
    attacks on British detention
        camps by, 64–65
    attacks on British
        government by, 67
    illegal immigration
        activities of, 69–71
    protects Jews in Palestine,
        51
    reaction to "Black
        Sabbath," 68
    sinks Patria, 54
    transformed into Israel
        Defense Forces (IDF), 81
Hall, George, 64
Hamid, Sultan Abdul, 34
Harrison, Earl G., 64
Hashomer Hatzair (socialist
    group), 43
Hatikvah (anthem), 74, 75
hats, worn by Jews, 15
Hebrew language, 38, 40, 50
Hebrews. See Jews
Hebrew University, 46
Hehalutz youth groups, 42–43
Herzl, Theodore
    commitment to Jewish
        nation, 28, 29
    considers Uganda
        proposal, 36–37
    death of, 37
    negotiates with Ottoman
        Empire, 33–34
    seeks allies for political
        Zionism, 30–31
    yields to Ahad Ha'am, 35
Hess, Moses, 24
Hirsch, Moritz de, 28
Histadrut (labor
    organization), 44–45
Hitler, Adolf
    Jews' fate under, 57–58
    role in Holocaust, 11
    writes Mein Kampf, 47
Holocaust, 11
    survivors
        Arabs empathize with, 88
        immigrate to Israel,
            87–88
Hovevei Zion groups
    colonization efforts of,
        26–27
    criticisms of, 27–28
    formed by Russian Jews, 24

support Herzl, 32
humor, wartime, 77
Husayni, Al-Haji al-, 72
Hussein (king of Jordan), 99

Imber, Naphtali Herz, 75
immigration to Israel
    housing and hardships,
        90–91
    Israel's commitment to,
        89–90
    map of, 92
    from 1948 to 1950, 87
    of Oriental Jews, 88–89
immigration to Palestine
    Anglo-American
        Committee report on, 66
    British restrictions on, 49,
        52, 55, 67
    illegal activities and, 48,
        69–71
    refugee ship efforts and,
        53–55
    see also aliyah
Innocent III (pope), 15
In the Year 1096 . . . The First
    Crusade and the Jews
    (Chazan), 14
Irgun, 57
    attack British detention
        camps, 64–65
    attack Deir Yassin, 72, 73
    outlawed by Ben-Gurion,
        81
    retaliates after "Black
        Sabbath," 68
    role in Altalena affair,
        79–80
    violent tactics of, 62
Israel, state of
    armies of, 94–95
    character of Jews born in,
        92–94
    conflicts among Jews in, 92
    conflicts with Arabs. See
        Arab-Israeli conflict
    economic crisis of, 97–98
    formal independence
        declared by, 74
    government of, 85, 86–87
    historic dates in creation
        of, 8–9
    map of, after June 10, 1967,
        94

1948 War of
  Independence, 74, 76–79
withdraws troops from
  Lebanon, 98
*see also* immigration to
  Israel
Israel Defense Forces (IDF),
  81
Israeli Jews, defined, 87
*Israelis, The* (Elon), 23
Israelites. *See* Jews

Jabotinsky, Vladimir, 45,
  46–47, 57
Jerusalem
  becomes international city,
    11
  map of old city, 49
Jewish Agency
  becomes representative of
    the Yishuv, 42
  protects Yishuv, 53
  pushes for Jewish army, 55
Jewish army, 55
Jewish Company, 33
Jewish defense groups. *See*
  Haganah; Irgun; Lehi
*Jewish State: An Attempt at a
  Modern Solution of the Jewish
  Question* (Herzl), 31–32
Jews
  Arab, 90
  Christian crusades against,
    13–15
  early myths about, 14–15
  economic discrimination
    against, 15–17, 20
  fate under Nazi rule, 57–58
  flee from Germany, 49–50
  history of, 13
  as moneylenders, 16–17
  19th-century emancipation
    of, 21–22
  numbers killed by Nazis, 62
  Oriental, 88–89, 90, 91–92
  racial definition of, 22
  reaction to Anglo-
    American Committee
    report, 66
  treatment in Poland, 17–18
  treatment in Russia, 19–20
  *see also* immigration to
    Israel; immigration to
    Palestine

Jordan, 84
*Judenstaat, Der* (Herzl), 31–32,
  33

Karay, Feliciya, 94
kibbutzim, 39
kibbutzniks, as soldiers, 77
King David Hotel, 68
Kishinev massacre, 35–36
Knesset (parliament), 85

Labor-Socialist coalition, 85
Law of Return, 87
League of Anti-Semitism, 21
Lebanon, war in, 97–98
Lehi, 57
  attacks British detention
    camps, 64–65
  attacks Deir Yassin, 72, 73
  members arrested, 83
  murders Lord Moyne, 61
  violent tactics of, 62
Lilienblum, M. L., 27
Louis IX (king of France), 15,
  18
*luftmenschen* (men of air), 19

maabaroth (camps), 91
maps
  Jewish relocation to Israel,
    92
  1948 Arab invasion of
    Palestine, 81
  1967 Israel, 94
  old city of Jerusalem, 49
  Pale of Settlement, 21
  Partition of 1948
    (Resolution 181), 11
Marr, Wilhelm, 21–22
martial law, 68–69
May Laws of 1882, 20
McMahon, Sir Henry, 41
*Mein Kampf* (Hitler), 47
Meir, Golda
  handles immigrant
    housing, 90–91
  immigrates to Palestine,
    42–43
  resigns as prime minister,
    95
military conscription, 19–20
Mizrachi Party, 38
Mohilever, Rabbi Samuel, 38
moshavim (co-ops), 39

Moyne, Lord, 61

Naguib, Muhammad, 82
National Military
  Organization. *See* Irgun
Nazis. *See* Hitler, Adolf
Netanyahu, Benjamin, 99
Nicholas I (czar of Russia),
  19–20
Nicholas II (czar of Russia),
  35
"Night of the Bridges," 67
Nobel Peace Prize, 96
Nordau, Max, 30–31, 36

Operation Magic Carpet, 89
Operation Peace for the
  Galilee, 97
*Ordinary Heroes* (Hay), 59–60
Oriental Jews, 88–89, 90,
  91–92
Orthodox Judaism, 86
Ottoman Empire
  crumbles during World
    War I, 40–41
  Herzl's negotiations with,
    33–34

Pale of Settlement
  creation of, 19
  description of, 23
  map of, 21
Palestine
  British plans for, 51
  call for new Jewish home
    in, 24
  falls under British rule, 41
  Hovevei Zion colonists in,
    24, 26–28
  in World War I, 40–41
  *see also* immigration to
    Palestine
Palestine Liberation
  Organization (PLO), 97
Palmach, 52
paratrooper missions, 58–59
parliament, Israeli, 85
Partition of 1948. *See*
  Resolution 181
Pasha, Azzam, 65
*Patria*, 53–54
Peel, Lord Robert, 51
Peres, Shimon, 98
Persian Gulf War, 98

Pinsker, Leo, 26, 27
PLO (Palestine Liberation Organization), 97
Poalei Zion Party, 38–39
pogrom (massacre), 20
poisoned water, 14
Poland, treatment of Jews in, 17–18, 56
Public Works Office, 44–45

Rabin, Yitzhak
  in *Altalena* affair, 80
  loses 1977 election, 96
  reelected as prime minister, 99
refugee ships, 53–55
Reines, Rabbi Isaac Jacob, 38
religious laws, 86
Resolution 181, 72
  map of partition, 11
Revisionist movement, 43, 46–47, 57
ritual murder, 14–15, 17
*Rome and Jerusalem* (Hess), 24
Rothschild, Baron Edmond de, 31–32, 41
Russia
  anti-Semitism in, 25
  treatment of Jews in, 19–20, 24
  Zionism in, 24, 26–28

Sabbath, 86
sabras (native Israelis), 92–93
Sadat, Anwar, 96
Sadeh, Yitzchak, 51
*Scattered Among the Nations* (Rubin), 18
Schiff, Friedrich, 30
Semites, 21
Seventh Zionist Congress, 37
Shamir, Yitzhak, 97–99
Shaw, Sir Walter, 49
Shaw Report, 49
shtetls (villages), 19
Sinai Campaign of 1956, 95
Six Day War, 95
Sixth Zionist Congress, 36–37
Smolenskin, Peretz, 24
Statute of Kalisz, 17

Stern, Avraham, 61
Stern Gang, 62
  *see also* Lehi
Szenes, Chana, 59

Talmud, 38
Tel Aviv, 77–78
Ten Days War, 82
Tenth Zionist Congress, 38
Torah, 12, 86
Transjordan, 82
"trucks-for-blood" affair, 60–61
Truman, Harry, 64, 65, 67
Trumpeldor, Joseph, 42

Uganda proposal, 36–37
Unger, Aviva, 87–88, 93–94
United Nations
  imposes second cease-fire, 82
  issues Resolution 181, 11, 72
  proposed role in Palestine, 66
usury, 16

wars
  1948 War of Independence, 74, 76–79
  Operation Peace for the Galilee, 97
  Six Day War, 95
  Ten Days War, 82
  Yom Kippur War, 95
Weinfeld, Miriam, 65
Weizmann, Chaim
  opposes Uganda proposal, 37
  as president of Israel, 85
  as president of Zionist Organization, 46
  reaction to terrorist tactics, 62, 68, 69
  relationship with Ben-Gurion, 56, 74
  role in "trucks-for-blood," 60–61
  testifies to Anglo-American Committee, 66
  viewed as "pushy Jew," 67

White Paper, 52
Wiesel, Elie, 59
Wingate, Orden, 51–52
Wolffsohn, David, 37–38
World War I, 40–41
World War II
  attempts to save Jews during, 58–59, 60–61
  beginning of, 52
  ending of, 62
  preserving the Yishuv during, 53, 55–56

Yadin, Yigael, 77–78
Yad Mordechai, 78
yekkes (German Jews), 49
Yiddish language, 40
Yishuv
  economic and technological growth of, 66
  industry in, 45
  old compared to new, 24
  sends paratroopers to Balkans, 58–59
  during World War II, 53, 55–56
Yom Kippur War, 95

Zangwill, Israel, 31
Zionism
  defined, 11
  history of, 23–24
  impact on Arab communities, 43–44
  official language of, 38
  Russian, 24, 26–28
Zionist Congress, First, 33–34
Zionist Congresses, 36–38
Zionist Organization
  becomes Jewish Agency in Yishuv, 42
  divisions within, 38–39
  function of, 33
  growth in, 37–38
  Weizmann elected president of, 46
Zionist youth groups, 43
Zion Mule Corps, 42

# Picture Credits

Cover photo: UPI/Corbis-Bettmann

Archive France/Tallandier/Archive Photos, 10, 57, 68, 73

Archive Photos, 28, 29, 30, 35 (top), 44, 45, 59, 62, 79, 84, 87

ASAP/GPO/Woodfin Camp & Associates, Inc., 60

Corbis, 20, 50

Corbis-Bettmann, 25

Daily Mirror/Corbis, 91

*Ein Bilderbuch für Gross und Klein*, Nuremberg, 1936/Simon Wiesenthal Center Archives, Los Angeles, CA, 22

*Historic Costume in Pictures*, Braun & Schneider, Dover Publications, Inc., © 1975, 14, 17

Library of Congress, 15, 16, 54

National Archives, 58

North Wind Picture Archives, 19, 35 (bottom)

Popperfoto, 36

UPI/Corbis-Bettmann, 12, 31, 46, 47, 63, 66, 67, 71, 76, 80, 83, 86, 89, 96, 98

Ricardo Watson/Archive Photos, 97

Yad Tabenkin Archives, 39, 51

# About the Author

Linda Jacobs Altman has written many books for children and young people, including *Amelia's Road*, the story of a young migrant farmworker, and *Genocide: The Systematic Killing of a People*. She has also written many books on Jewish topics for young people, including *Life on an Israeli Kibbutz* (Lucent) and *Forever Outsiders: Jews and History From Ancient Times to August 1935* (Blackbirch).

She lives with her husband, Richard, and an assortment of four-legged friends in Clearlake, California. When not writing she enjoys studying Spanish and collecting VHS movies.